GERALD DAVIES
An Autobiography

GERALD DAVIES

An Autobiography

London
GEORGE ALLEN & UNWIN
Boston   Sydney

First published in 1979

GEORGE ALLEN & UNWIN LTD
40 Museum Street, London WCIA ILU

© Gerald Davies, 1979

British Library Cataloguing in Publication Data

Davies, Gerald, b. *1945*
  Gerald Davies, an autobiography.
  1. Davies, Gerald, b. 1945
  2. Rugby football players – Wales
  – Biography
  796.33′3′0924   GV944.9.D/

  ISBN 0-04-796052-3

Typeset in 11 on 13 point Plantin by Northampton Phototypesetters Ltd and printed in Great Britain by W. & J. Mackay Ltd, Chatham

DEDICATION
To Cilla, Emily and Ben

Contents

Illustrations

Picture Credits

The author and publishers thank Sport & General for permission to use photograph no. 4; Colorsport for nos. 5–7, 9, 12–15, 19–24, and 27–38; Ken Davies for nos. 11 and 40; Michael Isaacs for nos. 16–18 and 26; Dennis Stephens for no. 25; the *Western Mail* for no. 39 and Reed Bingham for no. 41. The two Gren cartoons are reproduced by courtesy of Western Mail & Echo Ltd.

Part of pages 96–103 is abridged from the chapter entitled 'Wing' by Gerald Davies in *Rugby*, written and compiled by John Hopkins and published by Cassell Ltd in collaboration with Schweppes.

Preface

There are very many people to whom I am indebted and of whom there is no mention in this book. I am sorry if they look in vain for their names.

A host of people in Llansaint have given unwavering support throughout, whether verbally or by turning up by the minibus load to watch Wales or Cardiff play, teachers at school gave encouragement; there are those in the Carmarthen Athletic Club and Kidwelly RFC who have given me a consistently warm welcome whenever I have returned; the committee men of the Welsh Academicals gave me my first taste of a rugby club tour, and one of them was kind enough to suggest persuasively that an innocent youngster should not, repeat *not*, be tempted to try a 'three-man lift'; there are contemporaries and friends at Loughborough and Cambridge, committee men and supporters at London Welsh and Cardiff who gave assistance and the benefit of their knowledge and experience whenever and wherever it was needed; there are colleagues in every one of the three schools at which I briefly taught and in the Sports Council for Wales who must have felt put upon whenever I took leave of absence to play rugby, but there were no complaints – at least I did not hear of any.

To distinguish them as major or minor characters would be a grave injustice. What I have tried to do is to highlight what seemed to me significant milestones in my career as a rugby player. What they and countless others did was to allow me the opportunity to take part in a golden episode

in British rugby history, and to play with many great and
famous players:

>Born of the sun they travelled a short while toward
>>the sun,
>And left the vivid air signed with their honour.

GERALD DAVIES
An Autobiography

1

The separate bits and pieces of the crowded week never fell into a recognisable or predictable pattern. Certainly there was the office to go to and work to be done, but however good my intentions, I cannot pretend I gave it my undivided attention. Progress was staccato and never continuous, in the face of frequent interruptions. There were countless, well-wishing phone calls ('Just to wish you the best of luck. I don't think much of your opposite number'), innumerable casual chats and personal previews ('What are the chances, then? Do you think we'll make it?'), formal media interviews ('Gerald, this is your forty-third cap, and the fifth time you've played against this team at the Arms Park. How do you see it going?'), ticket collecting and distribution ('Could you leave them at the Athletic Club? I'll collect them at two').

People came and went, dropped in and out again, voices clicked on and off. Some were unknown and still are but for that brief moment. Long-forgotten acquaintances suddenly re-appeared as familiar friends: distant connections somehow assumed a firm bond (Close Encounters of the Heard Kind). Overnight, rugby balls and autograph books materialised like mushrooms on my empty desk, each accompanied by a brief cryptic note giving some sort of reason. Each tiny and inconsequential item was invaluable to someone and together they added up to something

I

never less than important to me. They were always anticipated, but when, how and where could they be fitted in? Other people's minutes grew into my hours.

The jigsaw took on an unmistakable, unchanging pattern on the get-together night, four or five days after the last Sunday squad session. Friday night was always enjoyably, excitingly the same. Thursday night too, for that matter, if it was an away match and we had to travel the following day. It was enjoyable because the week-long preliminaries were over, the superficial 'busy-ness' had taken on a controllable calm; exciting because we would all be together, with no distracting outside engagements and so much to look forward to. There was a sense of growing commitment. On Friday the parts finally started to fit perfectly, even if it was to an imperfectly timed routine. Between 5.30 and 6.00 pm we would drift in, in dribs and drabs, to sign in at the familiar, friendly Angel Hotel, comforting guardian of tomorrow's heroes and a hundred-yard sprint to the Arms Park. Walk through its pillared portals, sign in on the left, turn to collect the door key on the right.

'Key's in the door, sir.'

Through to the grandly chandeliered foyer to take the lift to the inevitable third floor. For me, it was always room 303. Then wait – wait for JPR, room-mate of a hundred different hotels. Room numbers changed, hotels had different names, but my room-mate remained the same from Perth to Pretoria, Tokyo to Toronto, Suva to Sydney, from Dublin to Dunedin and back – back to the Angel. We had shared that particular room for nine successive seasons since 1969, when he first burst on the scene, fearless, flamboyant, flowing hair and bare legs, socks strangely ungartered. He gave birth immediately, if not to records, certainly to club-house brain-teasers. Who played sixteen times for Wales in one season?* Who played for Wales as a back and as a forward?‡

'Room 303 again. It's about time they put a blue plaque on the door,' he said once, imperiously but with a hint of impish humour. That remark, too, became part of the routine towards the end. 'They still haven't put it up . . . ' Understood. But who should put it up? The Welsh Rugby Union? The Sports Council? Or perhaps the Royal College of Surgeons?

The last name may sound incongruous, but in fact JPR must have done most of his vital medical revision in that room. His most crucial hospital exams always had an awkward habit of turning up in the week after an Inter national match. Not that it mattered one iota to him, nor did it divert his single-minded attention from the immediate task in hand, but while I turned up on the eve of the match with what I considered to be a book of some literary merit, or a whodunnit, he invariably brought in some unwieldy tome of great medical importance. Such obligatory reading he lightened with the recent Alistair Maclean or Frederick Forsyth. It seemed an appropriate mixture for a man who shows a deep, conscientious concern for his vocation in general and sports injuries in particular, and who plays rugby with a derring-do that would flatter any thriller-writer's heroes!

6.00–6.30 pm. Time to turn down the corner of the page and watch and listen to the television pundits give their match previews and analysis. Fingers crossed for encouraging signs of good weather. A quick telephone call home to ensure that everything is fine.

---

*J. P. R. Williams (1968–69): 5 in Argentina, 4 home Internationals, 7 in New Zealand, Australia and Fiji.

‡J. P. R. Williams. He played at flanker in the Second Test in Australia in 1978.

6.30–7.00 pm. We search along the corridor for Gerry Lewis, the masseur. Among his many duties are the distribution of kit and invitation cards to tomorrow night's celebratory Dinner and Dance. Tonight it will be our shorts and red and white socks, all antiseptically clean, folded fresh, neat and tidy in a polythene bag. A shake of the hand. 'Size 30 waist, you said.'

'Yes, thanks.'

Not that it makes the slightest difference to me. I would always wear another, an already washed and worn pair for tomorrow's match. The pristine white pair will have to wait until they, too, have faded and feel comfortable. Call it superstitious, but most people in such circumstances prefer to do what is familiar and comforting.

For the moment there is no jersey. That revered and much sought-after garment will have to wait, wait for a different reason, for a different time. It has its own special moment of presentation, its own glorious part in the synchronised ritual.

'Don't forget now, boys. Dinner in fifteen minutes,' Gerry says, as if we need reminding. 'Then cinema.'

7.00–7.30 pm. Gareth Edwards inevitably joins JPR and me and just as inevitably he enquires whether there is a spare ticket handy. We move casually down to dinner. Our triumvirate, as the Press has termed it, is not in any way exclusive, or at least is not meant to be. It is merely that we are the most experienced, we have travelled many a mile together and the routine has gradually developed over the years. Imperceptibly at first, and before we knew it, it too had become part of the routine and we did it all the time. In the end it became something of an in joke amongst our team-mates and a table was purposely kept for us, just as if we were veteran members in a gentlemen's club.

'Hey,' whispers someone, as we stroll into the dining

room, 'here they come.' And a shade louder, 'Table ready for you, boys.'

'Oh, siwt mae, boys bach,' shouts the great bearded Viking that is Ray Gravell. 'De you're like wine ay. You get better as you mature.'

'Well,' retorts someone else before it all gets out of hand, 'will you listen to this wine connoisseur from Mynyddygarreg? Don't be fooled, Grav. JPR's with them because he's a doctor. OK, so he's not actually qualified in geriatrics but somebody's got to make sure the other two get to the ground tomorrow.'

Others join the table afterwards and a lot of banter and chat follow. Who's in, who's out. What happened to your club last week? You've got a good chance in the Cup this year. You can never tell, can you? Cup rugby is eighty-minute rugby; past performance is no real indication. Where did you go last International? Did you meet up with so-an-so? He asked about you. He'd won a bet or something, promised to buy you a drink. Stories begin to flow, mostly funny, especially if you have the likes of Geoff Wheel or Phil Bennett on your table.

'I was walking down Princes Street, morning of the Scottish match,' says Wheelo. 'These two blokes met, walking in opposite directions they were. They were covered from top to toe in red and white. Bobble caps, scarves, rosettes – you name it, they had the lot. Couldn't mistake them.

'"Hello, Dai," says one.

'"Hello, Wil," says the other. Both from the same village probably.

'"Up for the game, are you?"

'Seriously, I ask you. What else would they be doing in Edinburgh, in March, and dressed like that?'

The whole table laughs at Wheelo's story.

'They turned to me. "Hello, Geoff. Fit are you?" Have

5

you noticed they always ask you that on the morning of a match? "No," I answered. "Both legs broken getting out of bed this morning."

' "Oh, get on with you. You're orright," one of them said. "What'll it be? Thirty points? Ah well, all the best anyway, give 'em all you've got."

'And without waiting for an answer, off they both went, arm in arm, to a very pressing engagement at the Scottish and Newcastle.'

So the talk goes on. Benny talks of the time he missed the flight and was delayed in the space-age Charles de Gaulle Airport. Wheelo says he didn't want to go to New Zealand anyway: there was more fun down Swansea Docks on a Saturday night. Players, selectors, committee men all mix, talk, joke. There is no undue reverence because the Big Five are there: we are all part of the same thing. The spirit is usually casual, easy and good. Serious, tactical bits are thrown in occasionally, indicating a nervous edge just under the surface, but the adrenalin need not start flowing until tomorrow.

A glass of wine or beer helps the meal of soup, fish and steak go down well. In comes Gerry once again to get everybody together under his kindly, protective wing like a mother hen. 'Ten minutes! Meet in the foyer, OK? James Bond film tonight. That should please everybody, shouldn't it?'

8.15–8.30 pm. We make our way as a group down Duke Street, past the Castle and into Queen's Street towards a rendezvous with a movie. It's a busy night, with the weekend about to start. From the noise coming from some of the pubs, you would think that people were already starting to celebrate. People hurrying in the opposite direction, however urgent the appointment, stop and say in hushed tones, 'The Welsh team' as if there is only one Welsh team and one sport. 'There's Derek, Phil and Steve,' they say,

6

loud enough so we can hear, and turn our heads to confirm. Tonight we are all as familiar to them as next-door-neighbours and on first-name terms. Tomorrow, you see, will be a time for all of us and them to re-affirm our common cause, our common identity and our nationhood. Surnames will be back in fashion next week, when we will be back with our clubs and our side is playing theirs.

'C'mon, Reames, let's get a seat near Geoff. Even if the film's boring we're bound to have a few laughs,' says Gareth.

Huddled in our seats, clutching lollipops and choc-ices, we sit transfixed by the thud and blunder of Bond. It's no different from sitting in the stalls watching Buster Crabbe doing his Flash Gordon bit against Emperor Ming in the Saturday matinées long ago. Tomorrow the ninepenny stalls will give way to the exclusive North Stand debentures, and the goodies will be wearing red jerseys.

10.10 pm. We've walked the familiar route back and settled in the cushioned comfort of the Angel for tea and sandwiches. A few brief words, generally about the film, but: 'Boys bach, they've got no chance tomorrow, no chance at all – unless they kick off half an hour before us !' are Wheelo's parting words for the night.

Bond's fantastic adventures always nourish such feelings of elation and invincibility. Not a bad thing to sleep on.

There's nothing more to do or say but to go to bed.

★   ★   ★

There's a knock at the door. JPR gets up slowly, opens it and immediately falls back into bed, hardly checking on the person who wants to come in. He peers, bleary-eyed, at his watch. Nine o'clock. Nine-o'-blasted-clock.

'Good morning, boys,' chirps Gerry, sauntering gaily in. He has already started his relatively early morning round.

'Both all right? Sleep well?'

'Apart from the noise of the traffic, a couple of fire brigades and forgetting to turn off the central heating – apart from that OK,' I mumble from under my blankets.

'It's only nine o'clock, Gerry. Have a heart!' pleads JPR. He asks for some physiotherapy later on, then his head hits the pillow again.

'Yes, yes, of course. Weather's fine, it'll be a running game today,' says Gerry cheerily, hardly noticing our complaints. He has become accustomed to them over his years with the team and will encounter similar moans in other rooms on a match day. He details the morning timetable: '11.30 team talk, room 320. Lunch at 12, OK?'

Muffled noises from the two beds. Out goes Gerry to complete his round, keeping everyone informed and treating the needy, especially the sensitive, 'piano-playing' backs. The routine has begun.

Left alone, we turn uneasily in our beds. We try to grab some more rest, but it's a futile hope. We both know that the day has started and it's going to be a long morning. Best, though, to keep away from the milling crowds downstairs in the hotel foyer, and bed is as good a place to be as any.

The telephone rings.

'There are supposed to be no calls before eleven. Didn't you tell the receptionist?' grumbles JPR.

'I thought you did that.'

I pick up the receiver. 'Is that you, Del?' enquires the anonymous and out-of-breath voice at the other end.

'No, wrong room.'

The voice is not deterred. It asks: ''Aven't got any tickets by any chance, 'ave you?'

'No!'

Down goes the receiver. It is the first of many such calls. At this point let's turn the clock back, back to an

Edinburgh hotel room during Clive Rowlands' reign as coach. That was when the success began, and when Clive brought his own flavour and fervour to pre-match team talks. At 11.25 on the morning of the match, the room would be gradually filling as the players arrive. Some are earnest-looking, some joking. Most look untidy, their flowery shirts lack the matching ties and are open to the chest. But Shadow – Dai Morris to the Bob Bank crowd – who was up early and who, alone, has dared venture into the town, is immaculate in a clean yellow shirt and carefully knotted Barbarians tie.

There's plenty of colourful talk, too: staccato sentences from the nervous new members, relaxed and light-hearted conversation and banter among the experienced. Out of the hubbub one voice (from the front-row union, of course) rises above the rest, to enquire of Gareth Edwards about the health of the 'King', Barry John, and to ask what it is like to share a room with him. The 'King', Gareth reports, is shaving. The front-row union express mock surprise that the 'King' is performing this humble task himself: 'Can't quite be royalty yet, then.'

'You wait,' says Gareth, quick as a flash, 'you wait till he cuts himself – the blood comes out blue orright!'

John 'Mr Greedy' Lloyd comes in and asks for his mate, Shadow. 'Sign these,' he says. 'They're for the boys at school.' He passes over some autograph books, miniature footballs and a motley collection of hotel paper and menus to be circulated among the players.

The room is now nearly full, both of smoke (although only Clive Rowlands has a cigarette) and of bodies. Both beds are in danger of collapsing; one of them supports the weight of five forwards, as well as Phil Bennett, a reserve to-day, huddling uncomfortably between the mighty shoulders of his fellow sospans, Del Thomas and Barry Llewellyn. The other players are lying all over the floor.

9

'Everybody here, then?' says Clive. 'Good. On time too.'
Somebody corrects him – one player is missing.
'Where's John Bevan? Not still in bed is he? Keith, go
and get him. Tell him to hurry – a minute to go.' Clive
parades up and down what little space there is left in the
room, puffing at his cigarette.

Ray Williams, the coaching organiser, walks in and is
reminded that he is only just in time. Dapper he is, in a
lightweight suit. 'New suit, Ray?' someone shouts from the
overloaded bed.

'Yes. Smart eh?'

'Very nice. Pity they didn't have it in your size though.'
Everybody laughs.

'Cheeky!'

John Bevan rushes in and apologises to Clive.

'You're lucky,' says Clive. 'You had two seconds to spare,
else it would've been fifty press-ups.' No-one is sure whether
he is joking. 'Orright. Turn the radio off. Out here, Gareth.
Let's have a shout. Let's get a proper frame of mind.'

Out comes Gareth to the front, to the tiny space, to
simulate the call for the first scrum. 'On the call then, boys
. . . together . . . ready . . . steady, Jeff. Ball in . . . *now*!'
And there's a chorus of noise.

'Not good enough,' insists Clive. 'Do it again.'

'Hold it then,' says Gareth, already crouched as if in the
real match, putting the real ball into the first real scrum.
'Hold it, Jeff. Ball in . . . *now*! And again the chorus, backs
and forwards alike, shouting to raise the roof.

'Better, better. Once more,' says the familiar gruff
voice. The accumulated cigarette ash droops. Once more
Gareth coaxes the imaginary first scrum. 'Great, great,'
comes the reward from Clive. 'Now we're together.' And
there is seriousness and total silence in the cramped room
as the ash from his cigarette falls and disintegrates on the
floor. Clive begins to talk.

'This match is important. It's important that we win and win well. We haven't come all this way to lose. Think' – there's nothing else to do in that room now – 'think of your families at home, of your friends who've travelled up to see you play. And not only to see you play, but to see you win. For Wales. Do you know,' he says, 'do you know what I saw in the hotel foyer just now?' We are listening intently for the little anecdote that he unfailingly provides, either quoting a misguided pressman to make us angry, or giving an example of some people demonstrating their unashamed patriotism to make us even more emotional, to make the ticker tick that little bit faster. 'There they were,' he goes on ''alf a dozen of them, walking into the hotel, one of them with a telly under his arm. Imagine it, a TV – "Just in case we don't get a ticket, see, Clive." You may think it funny. But that's enthusiasm for you boys. They're all there behind you, willing you on to win. 15,000 of them have travelled all the way up here to see Wales win. For those at home in Cefneithin, there's no stop-tap this afternoon. And if you win there's an extension till five tomorrow morning.' Silence. Phil, bunched between Llew and Del, smiles at this. The King smiles too, but no more than that. 'Now come on.' Clive drags out those last two words. 'We haven't travelled all this way for nothing. No fear. We've come to beat them, and in their own territory. We're the best in Europe. We've proved it. And we're going to prove it again this year. We're going to win. What are we going to do, Jeff?'

'Win,' comes the reply, almost apologetically.

'What?' asks Clive aggressively.

'Win.' A little louder this time but still half-heartedly.

'Can't hear you. What did you say?' Goading him this time.

'WIN!' he bellows. They must hear it in Cefneithin.

'That's better. Let's hear it next time. It's going to be

hard. We've got to take the game to them, we mustn't let them get on top. That first ten minutes is vital. Vital. They're going to come at us like bats out of hell. So in the scrums and lineouts we must have tight control. Go down in the scrums together, all eight, tight. Right, Jeff? No penalties, no nonsense. Right?

And on he goes, his emotive voice brandishing words like an old-time evangelist, picking on individual players: Gareth to have good ball, Barry to control it, Arthur Lewis to tackle, tackle, tackle; wings get back, help in defence to start the counter. Oh, we've got to win, we must win. For our friends, for our country – for Wales.

'It's vital, vital. My ticker is going like the clappers.' He thumps his chest with the cigarette-free hand. 'We've got to win. We must win.' The sweat is running down his face. 'What are we going to do, John? What are we going to do, Mr Greedy? Eh?'

'Win.'

'Yes, yes. And if your opposite number gets anywhere near you, what will you do? What will you do?'

'I'll . . . ' he stutters, 'I'll . . . I'll eat him!'

Silence. Phil is the first to giggle, then Barry, then Jeff and finally the whole room erupts with laughter. Clive, leaning forward, hands on his knees, is choking himself.

Mr Greedy looks incredulous and insists, 'I will beat him. Wales will beat them all.'

*   *   *

Players have come and gone. Those were high, bright days, days of Shadow, the King, Mr Greedy and Delme. But 'Sid' Dawes, who was then captain, is now coach and the success has continued. The qualities Sid once had as leader are still there. He is cool and calculating, more analytical at this stage than Clive in what he has to say. He seems above the situation, but occasionally the feelings of the expatriate Welshman come through, in quoting what they have to say in England, in reporting what question marks, what doubts they have about the present Welsh side. Whatever the opposition, it is time to prove again and again how good we are: there is an almost desperate need to disprove the cynics.

The details have been ironed out in training sessions. What happens in room 320 of the Angel Hotel on that Saturday morning is a gentle reminder, to make sure that we are clear in our minds, with general comments about the players, theirs and ours, the strengths and the weaknesses. It is no longer a performance with a theatrical face to it: what Clive used to say to engender the right feeling is now deeply embedded in us all, and Sid's quieter approach is a natural progression. We are happy with it.

12 noon. The team talk over, the players make their own way down in their own time to lunch in the Foxhunter Room, named after Sir Harry Llewellyn's four-footed Olympian. The ladies are already there to serve us. There's a huge tureen of soup, platters of fish and steak, bowls of chips and other vegetables. It's a bit of fish for me, some have steaks. Doctor JPR offers professional advice: 'Don't eat meat. It'll take twenty-four hours to digest. It won't do you any good.'

Even though he has said this time and time again, some of the players still ignore the advice. They will do what they want to do, what they have always done in the past. You cannot change the routine at this late stage. Ray Prosser from Pontypool, however, has already got the message through to his 'favour-right' four. Some time ago, it seems, he gave the same advice, but in his usual more pictorial, more colourful way. 'Give a lion a meal,' he said, 'and he'll go to sleep. Keep him hungry and he'll go hunting all day.' Beatrix Potter had said something on the same lines about lettuce having a 'soporific' effect on rabbits, although this was probably said more politely and with more decorum than Pross; as the legendary man is so often quoted as saying, 'I've no time for long words like "marmalade" and "corrugated". ' And as he so often does, he got to the root of the matter without the frills and the fuss. At any rate the Pontypool front row has heeded his call. They won't eat anything at this time of day. They still order their steaks, though, and when the meat arrives they pack it carefully in their serviettes to eat in the hotel room after the match – unless their wives get to them first.

Some players have curious eating habits on a match day. Brian Thomas, the Neath lock-forward, would have nothing more than a pound of grapes. Stranger still was Max Wiltshire who enjoyed a curry in mid-morning; whenever he travelled away he always took with him a Vesta pack, just in case we stayed in a hotel that was sub-standard and did not employ a chef who was familiar enough with the culinary arts of the East!

There are no such exotic requests in this Welsh team. Cups of sweet tea are ordered, toast and honey consumed, but there is no serious eating as such. Like children who would rather be out of doors than sitting impatiently at a table wasting valuable playing time, we pick at our food: a little bit of this, a little bit of that. The adrenalin which was missing last night is beginning to flow.

Programmes are dished out by the ever-present Gerry and read diligently. The pen portraits are the main targets for attention. The obvious outlet for nervous energy is leg-pulling and repartee.

'Oh, look at this photograph. Look at the sideboards. That was taken five years ago.'

'Hey, Charlie, your age hasn't changed since you were first capped three years ago.'

'Ah,' replies Charlie Faulkner, in his nasal Pontypool

drawl, 'it was a misprint then. I've nearly caught up with them now.'

'Well, look at this,' says JJ. 'They've got me down as a rep. Things have changed. I'm an area sales and personnel co-ordinator now!'

The waitresses come round again, offering more food, but find few takers. 'No, thanks. Tea and honey, please.' They're patient, though, because they know that the portly selectors will be in shortly and will gobble up the lot.

12.30 pm. Back to our rooms we go once more, to watch the match previews and Bob Wilson's soccer round-up on 'Grandstand'. If the timing is good, we can switch over to 'World of Sport' and watch the soccer there, too. There are last callers for tickets but they don't stay long. Time to prepare our bags. Shorts, socks, jockstrap, towel. All in. JPR's cleaned his boots. Albert, the Cardiff groundsman, will have mine ready when I get there.

'Ready, JPR?'

'OK. Let's go.'

Out of room 303, press the button for the lift. It comes.

'Oh, hold it for a minute. I've forgotten my gum-shield.' I must have that. Once Gareth forgot his in Paris, and he only remembered when we were already entombed in the Parc des Princes changing rooms. The police went back to fetch the missing object. It was an achievement worthy of the ingenuity of a nation that produced Maigret. In the classic manner of fiction they arrived back one minute before we were due to take the field – with the gum-shield.

Down we go to face the crowd in the foyer. As the lift door opens there is a sea of enthusiastic faces to greet and cheer us. 'Sign here, please': the autograph signing begins. A mixture of North and South Wales accents co-mingle, as do the Welsh and English languages. The nation is one today.

There's Mrs Edwards and the genial, ever-smiling Mr

15

Edwards, mother and father of GOE. 'Oh, dere ma', come here, Ger bach. Pob lwc heddi. Good luck,' she says every time I see her, here in the foyer. I know she means it down to the very last syllable, and he feels it down to his marrow. A miner all his life, and still is, just like my father was. Looking at Mr Edwards, I think of my own father and wish to God that he was here to savour all our recent magnificent success, to be part of this golden chapter of Welsh rugby history. The whole nation basks in the reflected glory and relishes it with pride, which is not a bad thing, not a bad thing at all. But I just wish, oh, I do wish that he could put his feet comfortably up and do the same. He read the preface in 1971 but the pages have been turned and what has become an unforgettable chapter has been written. He has gone, but I wish that he had been able to read it to the end.

'Pob lwc, Ger bach,' says Mr Edwards. In his eyes I see my father's eyes. Both miners, both had known suffering and hardship. Saturday afternoon's rugby match was the time for my father to get some of the floating coal-dust out of his lungs, to stretch those limbs which had remained cramped and closeted for hours on end in a tiny, dirty black hole. With the wind in his hair, breathing clean air and feeling the springy turf, he had played too. For me, in today's jargon, it is a recreational leisure activity; for him it was a great escape, an indispensable safety-valve.

'Hey, Ger, sign this will you?' From underneath a bobby-dazzler of a bobble cap comes another request to sign a £5 note. From the signatures on it I gather that most of my team-mates have already come this way and are now in the seclusion of the Arms Park. Where's my wife? My mother? I must see them before I leave this bustling, jostling crowd.

From behind: 'You've got your gum-shield, have you?' No ordinary fan this, she's too concerned for my well-being. So I turn round for a few final words with Cilla, who is with my mother and my two sisters, Mair and Elizabeth. I kiss them all, and they wish me luck.

Somehow, I meet up with Gareth and JPR. No stopping now. No time for autographs. Pleadings are given short shrift. We've got to go. Westgate Street has been blocked to traffic. There's much to-ing and fro-ing but hastily we make our way to the Cardiff and Wales Home Dressing Room. A hundred yards it may be to the ground but a sprint it most certainly is not, not today.

Outside the dressing room Bill McLaren is waiting for Gareth and hands him the boiled mint sweets from Hawick. That has been part of the ritual between the two of them, just as it has been his habit to refer to me on the air as 'this little man'. Eric Roberts, bus conductor and fully paid-up member of Plaid Cymru, prospective candidate for Jim Callaghan's constituency in Cardiff, is the man who guards the door of our changing room today and every International Saturday. In we go. Gareth goes to his usual peg immediately to the left, JPR goes to the far left-hand corner and predictably joins the forwards. I join Gareth. Most of the players are already there.

1.45 pm. 'Let's inspect the pitch,' suggests a voice. Out we all go together, down beneath the North Stand, past the strolling policeman, turn left at Bill Hardiman the WRU groundsman's room and through the large wrought-iron gates. We emerge onto the pitch to the accompaniment of loud cheers. But it's not as loud as it used to be. The North Enclosure, which was customarily full by this time, is virtually empty these days. There are seats now instead, and those with tickets rarely turn up until half an hour before kick-off: a place guaranteed, and no singing to while away the time. What remains of the North Enclosure has been relegated to the corner at the Taff End and merges with the West Terrace. There they wave their banners or anything red they can get their hands on. 'JPR doctors Englishmen' reads one, 'Charlie's my darling' another, 'Gravell eats soft centres' yet another. We acknowledge them, and throw little tufts of grass into the air to measure the strength and the direction of the wind. No advantage. There's nothing worse than a wind: it gives you a forty-minute advantage one way and a forty-minute struggle the other.

Back we go, and file underneath the yawning jaws of the North Stand. Bill Hardiman is there, proud as Three Feathers. It is time for him to relax; the weeks of tender care have brought their satisfying reward. The turf will be immaculate. When we arrive back in the dressing room Gerry is proudly distributing the treasured jerseys.

'Congratulations,' he says, as he holds out the garment in one hand and shakes your hand with the other. 'Many more of them.'

For this, countless Welshmen would willingly be born again. It is what children dream of. It is the glory of which a nation will passionately sing: the scarlet jersey of Wales. There is the proud rose of England, the subdued nobility of the thistle, the fragile dignity of the shamrock, but there is something powerfully majestic in Three Feathers which arouses a Welshman's passion. I wonder whether the others arouse similar emotions.

Gareth looks at his jersey, kisses the emblem and hangs it up on his peg.

There is now a growing sense of urgency, although there is still humour enough fluttering about the dressing room. Pricey has already been on Gerry's table, his shoulder and back red with deep heat mixed with Gerry's own special 'speed-oil' potion.

'Who's next on the table, Gerry?' shouts Bobby.

'Panther next, then JPR, then you.'

But that order will have to change. Inevitably, im-

18

patiently, Gareth will jump the queue, and Panther Martin will soon find himself relegated to the end if he is not careful.

'Oh, you piano-playing backs get all the favours. What about us donkeys? Don't we ever get preferential treatment?' he complains, but good-humouredly, with no hint of malice. Out he goes, all legs and arms, like the Pink Panther after whom he was nicknamed, out of the crowded, oil-bespattered floor of the dressing room. In the empty shower area he does his loosening-up exercises, jogging, arms akimbo, occasionally jumping for the lineout ball that is not there yet.

2.15 pm. Players are getting ready now, all at different stages of undressing. One or two are in a hurry and have all their kit on, looking swank; some are walking around in shorts looking for bandage; some are in jockstraps and socks, waiting for Gerry's ministrations. Benny is in the corner fully clothed, except for jacket and tie. He's a quick changer. No fuss and palaver for him: get 'em off and get 'em on in five minutes flat.

The Welsh Rugby Committee come in to wish people luck. The selectors do the same, and so do the coaching organisers, Ray Williams and his assistant, Malcolm Lewis. But Ray has something else up his sleeve. 'Try this,' says he, and dishes out bottles of orange-coloured liquid that tastes like Lucozade but is thicker and sweeter.

'What is it?' shouts someone. 'Shampoo for dandruff or what?'

'It gives you energy,' says Ray.

'Hey boys, Ray's putting us on drugs for us to play better,' calls a wag from a distant corner. 'You didn't mention this in your coaching manual. Secrets from the RFU, is it?'

'It'll help you wingers to maul better and you props to side-step.'

This is about the last attempt at humour. By now nobody is really listening. The referee comes in to check the studs, and the dressing room is gradually emptying except for the people that really matter from now on: the players, replacements, Gerry and his assistant.

Terry Cobner, man of few words, is sitting silently contemplating in the corner, deep in his own treasured thoughts. What goes on behind that inscrutable face? He's reminding himself, perhaps, of Pross's final instructions and conjuring up a few of his own. He smiles a broad, happy smile when someone passes and wishes him luck. 'Ay OK,' is all he says. He'll have plenty to say, though, when he has the other seven with him in his private conclave later on, with fifteen minutes to go. And he'll end by saying something like 'We'll either come back into this dressing room at half past four a bunch of buggers, or we'll play and come back a bunch of heroes. That's the choice.' He for one will come back a hero, as he has always done in every game he has played.

The smell in the dressing room is strongly of liniment and eucalyptus, a sure cure for nasal congestion. Gerry's table, after all the bodies that have been on it, is as slippery as a ski slope and anyone going on it now would be in danger of sliding off on the other side. The noise is the nervous chatter of players and the clacketty clatter of studs on the floor. In the deeper recess of this stand we cannot hear the crowd, but we know that they are in full throat. There is continuous movement, nobody stays still for a moment. Some are jogging or doing stretching exercises, warming up the delicate hamstrings; some dab vaseline on their knees, Vick on their chests and chins.

Above the hubbub Grav is singing, singing the old, familiar Dafydd Iwan refrain:

'A phawb o fewn ein gwlad yn siarad Cymraeg'.

Grav is all hustle and bustle, near panic, but Dafydd's

melody consoles and reassures him, restores in him the confidence which he needs, revives in him the sense of occasion
in which he is going to play his part. As Carwyn James once
said, no Welshman has ever played for Wales with a deeper
sense of being a Welshman.

2.35 pm. Twenty-five minutes to go. Time for a photograph outside on the adjoining Cardiff pitch, followed by
a run up and down the field to stretch our limbs and
breathe the fresh air. Then back to the dressing room,
while Benny goes for the toss-up and comes back happy in
the knowledge that he's already won something this
afternoon. Although there is no favourite way of playing
and no wind advantage, he says, 'We'll play towards the
scoreboard.'

We gather round Benny. 'Time for talking is over. It's
action now. Let's go out and do it,' he says.

Even though we are now in earnest, those phrases will
trigger off one particular memory in most of us. Once,
down in an Afan Lido squad session, when preparation
was seriously under way for the next match, 'Sid' Dawes
had been analysing the opposition's strengths and weaknesses, there were tactical talks and discussion. Gareth
suddenly stood up, sleeves rolled up, fists clenched, and
said, 'C'mon boys, time for talking is over. Let's go out
and do it.' Inspired, we all stood up and trooped out for
yet another work-out in the mud. And what did Gareth do?
Jumped onto Gerry's table and said, 'Can I have a rub
down, Gerry, please?' The forwards, particularly Bobby
Windsor, relish recapturing the moment.

But this is not the moment to linger on it and savour it.
'All together,' says Benny. 'Concentration and discipline.
Let's get down there. Let's play the game in their half,
especially the first twenty minutes. Pressurise them.' Short,
succinct phrases, reminding us of what we have done in
training, what we have talked about, what we should and

must do. 'C'mon lads. We're the Welsh team. Be proud of the jersey.' Very little tactical talk now – at 2.45 it is mainly emotional stuff, stirring the heart. This is no time for a rational appraisal of the likely pattern of the game. Benny paints a broad canvas. He knows how to string the words together, too. The words come out in a breathless, quick-fire fashion, throwing names of the lads in now and again. And when it is all over, Cob takes his own magnificent seven with him. They will not let him down this afternoon. He will lead by example, and his standard is high.

2.50 pm. A few more precious minutes to go. Everyone is warming up in earnest. We do it together, jogging on the spot. 'All together, one to ten then, lads,' and we raise the knees to the count of ten. Shoulders rolling next, then back and fore, stretching the fragile hamstrings. Back to a jog, raising a sweat.

'C'mon then, lads. Another count to ten.'

'All the best, Charlie.'

'All the best, Jeff. Just like New Zealand.'

'Have a good 'un, JJ.'

Someone peeps round the door. 'They're going out now.'

'OK. Last sprint to ten, then.'

2.55 pm. We're ready to go out, too. 'C'mon lads. We're on our own, now. Let's go.'

We troop out, one after another, underneath the North Stand. We reach the end of the concrete tunnel as the last of the opposition disappears through the gates that lead onto the field. Purposely we pause for a moment as the crowd quietens down. 'All the best,' says someone, finally. Out we go, into a sea of red and white. The cheers are almost tribal. 'WA-LES, WA-LES.'

This is what the waiting has been for. Throughout the week it has been a time to dream, a time to talk, but now is the time to act. For me the tension gives way to a sense of relief and relaxation because now we can go out and play. Concentrate on that and that alone. It is a good feeling to be alone, all, all alone on a wide expanse of grass that is the rugby theatre, the focus of all of Wales. Stand still, stand still. There is a hush as the band strikes up . . . . . 'M-ae H-en wl-ad F-y Nh-adau' . . . I wish I could say that I sing better here than anywhere else, but there is something which always sticks at the back of my throat and which doesn't let me. And it won't go away.

2

The past is a foreign country, they do things differently there.
L. P. Hartley: The Go-Between

Llansaint, the village where I was born, is a tiny, almost isolated place, situated prominently to overlook Carmarthen Bay. Not all maps acknowledge its existence, but if you do get hold of one which is suitably accurate you will find Llansaint clutched between the two claws of the Gwendraeth and Towy Rivers that with the Taf form a crowsfoot of estuaries flowing into the bay that eventually becomes the Bristol Channel. To travel by road, which is the only means of getting there, presents no small difficulty. For the village's one and only sighting, the coastal trunk road from Llanelli to Carmarthen needs to be followed to a long, flat stretch of road beyond Burry Port which is commonly known in the locality as the Pembrey Flats. From this point, look up to the north-west and you can see high up on the hill in the distance a prominent tower with a few whitewashed houses scattered along its base. You will need to be quick about it, though, because a few hundred yards further on the village disappears altogether from view into the undulating countryside, as if it had been an optical illusion in the first place.

For the average motorist that could be the end of it, since

24

unless he has a mind to he will not catch sight of the place again. Even if he has a mind to, he will find it difficult to get there for there are no signposts to indicate its whereabouts until he is well off the beaten track. In years gone by there were precious few who cared, although today it is fast becoming something of a haven to those who have been 'long in city pent'. Its qualities of solitude and obscurity which tended to put visitors off in the past are nowadays the very qualities that attract them there. But they must be on their guard and must not be too hasty: a headlong rush to get there can only frustrate and send them speeding back whence they came, feeling grateful for the clearly directed routes of the city. In the past the few people who went there arrived in the village by chance. The only intentional visits were made by the occasional bus, by relatives or by people who had something to sell.

Llansaint is flanked by the small fishing hamlet of Ferryside on one side of the hill and the twelfth-century town of Kidwelly on the other. The latter is famous for its splendid concentric castle, the legend of Gwenllian, its brickworks and its rugby team. Because of my association with the latter rugby club, Llansaint, to the villagers' immense disapproval, has never quite managed to be as famous as Gwaun cae Gurwen has been for Gareth and Cefneithin for Barry. Kidwelly throughout the year is a busy small town. Down below on the other side, Ferryside is a quiet seaside village for most of the year except during the summer months when it is transformed and becomes particularly active with yachtsmen and holidaymakers. For years none of this seemed to touch Llansaint. The folks who lived up on the hill were left very much to their own devices as there was nothing much to attract anybody there. Kidwelly and Ferryside are connected not only by a road which bypasses Llansaint but also by the Great Western Railway built in the middle of the last century.

Gerald Davies

Llansaint has a population of about 400 people. The centrepiece is the tower I have already mentioned, the thirteenth-century church of the Saints, which is the English translation of the village name, Llansaint. The tower also served as a beacon to warn shipping of the treacherous sands of Cefn Sidan. This did not always prove to be successful, as the number of shipwrecks which have occurred there testify. The remains of HMS *Paul* are still there for all to see, a shaky skeleton of its former shape.

Weatherbeaten though it is, facing bravely as it does the blasts of the prevailing south-westerly winds, Llansaint has avoided the ravages which could so easily have affected it had it been situated a hundred feet below at sea level. The havoc that can be caused by sea and storm did come that way once. The sea came in one night in the seventeenth century and the village of Hawton, built at sea level, was drowned never to recover. It was mainly as a result of that storm that the size of the village population increased. Those that survived retired to the hills not merely for comfort but for safety. Ever since, the sea has been less a source of livelihood, more a source of distrust; the rich fertile land that once was there was never reclaimed and in time it turned to sand. The village has never been known as a fishing community, although a few of the women would venture with their donkeys down to the shoreline to pick cockles and mussels.

The first houses quite naturally were built around the church in the village square and the small streets shoot off in all directions like the spokes in a wheel. Once in the village square it is as if in a maze to try to choose which way to go out again. On occasions it was the height of midsummer madness to see the cars that had drifted into the village; some curious tourist, perhaps, straying off the beaten track in search of local colour, or a pair of lovers trying to find a secluded spot in which to stray. They would

26

go round the church and off down one street, only to return to the very same spot. It was only through trial and error that they would ever find their way out again. As children, if asked for a direction, we would mischievously add to the confusion by misdirecting them. By the time they returned the street urchins would have conveniently disappeared. The shape of the village has not changed and very few houses have been built over the years as there has been no need. The population figures have remained roughly the same.

As Llansaint was a rural community the men were in the main agricultural labourers, or failing that they would travel long distances and become miners. Whichever one of these they did, and there were occasions when there was no choice whatsoever, it meant long arduous hours of physically demanding work. My father did both jobs at different times. Quite clearly, he preferred the former as it meant that he worked above the ground and in the fresh air. But jobs were few and far between and most of his working life was spent underground. It meant getting up very early in the morning and travelling seven miles to work. He first had to walk a mile and a half from the village down to the railway track and then catch a train to Glyn Hebog colliery. There were times during the winter when he literally did not see daylight at all except for the weekends. Because of the journey to the colliery he had to be up during the hours of darkness and the sun would be just about rising by the time he reached the colliery face. By the time he was up again the sun had gone down.

As a result, he never wished anything of the kind on me. For the most part my parents did much to protect me from any awareness of many of the hardships they had suffered. But they never failed to emphasise that if I did not stick to my education then I would inevitably follow my father down the pits. My father loved sport, for instance, but how many times he told me that spending too much time playing it would lessen my chances of gaining a good enough education so that I would not have to follow in his footsteps. He felt that I might suffer serious injury, and he had broken a few bones in his body in his time, and that this might delay or even halt my education. At this stage, therefore, a good education was of prime importance, with rugby a poor second. But for a child, to be out playing in the company of his own group is more important and more tangible than education, and to play rugby in Wales is such stuff as dreams are made on.

The community that once was static has become more fluid these days as communications to and from the village have improved. Then, the village population rarely changed from one decade to another. The odd person would drift away but it was always an isolated case and it would be a talking point for years until he would return. There was once a Llansaint man who in his teens packed up his bags, on the spur of the moment it seems, and went to sea. He was never seen for decades but was known to have settled in New Zealand. It was in 1969, when Wales toured that country, that I was standing in the foyer of a New Plymouth hotel on the morning of the match with Taranaki, when a hesitant, half-embarrassed voice, wishing to test the temperature more than anything, asked in Welsh, 'Y crwt o Llansaint?' ('The lad from Llansaint?') And I turned round to meet the man who was once the teenager who created the village legend. I was the first of several generations to have ever set eyes on him. I met him again in 1971. Thereafter he made up his mind to come home and see his parents. And he did. More than that, for a legend needs to perpetuate itself, he came back and married the sweetheart of his youth.

Another man went away and became the Bishop of Bangor. He was a legend, too.

With the coming of free grammar school education, the drift from the village started to speed up. In order to gain appropriate qualifications a young man or woman had to go away, and once having gone away there was no means by which he could come back to make even an adequate use of those qualifications. Jobs in the area other than the Church and teaching were simply not available. Education was highly valued and consistently encouraged but indirectly this was an encouragement, a passport even, to go away from the village. For a while it seemed that the village would ultimately die for there was a high percentage of passes for the eleven-plus and passes in further examinations after that. There was no-one to take the place of those who left. But in recent years the whole thing has tended to even itself out: some of the young are moving away, some prefer to stay to work for one of the light industrial firms or local authority offices which have established themselves in the district in recent years. The choice is more of an individual one these days and is less imposed. Better still, perhaps, is the fact that people from outside are moving in and contributing substantially to the life of the small community. There are very few holiday homes as such, so that the village life remains fairly constant throughout the year.

If you are born and bred in a closely knit country village with very little communication with the outside world, there are very few distractions. But the qualities of remoteness and inaccessibility had a double edge: whilst there was the occasional yearning for some closer contact with the outside world, for the most part as children we enjoyed and relished our independence. There was all the opportunity in the world to play, and sport had an important part in our lives. Rugby, soccer and cricket were played by the children in and out of season. If the Lions were playing or the MCC were overseas, what matter if it were summer or winter? Sport captured the attention regardless of the season and with sufficient imagination facilities could always be made readily available – after all the roads and the streets were our playground. The Council had provided us with a field but except during the summer months when the weather was fine and the field dry we rarely used it, so that instead the tarmacadam roads became the famous playing grounds of the world. Many a cricket Test match, cup final or rugby International was played out in the narrow streets of Llansaint. Traffic in and out of the village was rare, and since at times the only interruption was the bus which came along half a dozen times a day there was little danger to life and limb. Without too much exaggeration, we knew when play would be stopped by the bus company's time-table, and we would clear the roads accordingly. When street lighting came to the village what else would this mean but that we could play under floodlights? So whereas later in my rugby career I thought that floodlights were a bane and provided unnatural playing conditions for the game, in my much younger days I thought that street lighting was a boon. It simply meant an extension to playtime.

The sound of a ball bouncing on the road or banging against a wall would attract the attention of the children. The doors of the houses would open, as I imagine they did in Hamelin town when the Pied Piper played, the children would come out and we would pick up sides. Playing in a confined space as we often did, we had to adjust the rules of the game to suit the circumstances. Improvisation was the key word. In cricket, for instance, there was never more than one bat available, and there were pavements and walls in the way. So with the child's ingenuity we devised new rules for the game so that to hit the pavement would be one run, four runs if we hit the wall beyond. The greatest obstacles of course were the well-tended gardens, with their prized vegetables. To hit the ball in there was clearly six and out. Six indicated that we recognised it was a wonderful feat but the offender had to go out since we might never see a ball again. The skilful culprit suffered further ignominy and embarrassment by having to go in and retrieve the ball from the greenery.

The men in the village jealously guarded their gardens; spring and early summer was a time of sporting contest in the village. Men bragged about their early potatoes, boasted about the length of their runner beans and, whilst they had divided loyalties over rugby and soccer, the vegetable contest was common ground, as it were. Men who were unemployed or severely disabled, usually from pneumoconiosis, devoted a lot of their time to looking after the gardens. It not only provided family fare, it also aroused passionate debate on the pros and cons of various methods of cultivation and there was great controversy as to who could produce the first lot of vegetables in season. It was not uncommon for a man actually to buy the vegetables from the market and bring them home to boast as if they were his own produce.

It was this passion, then, that we were wary of when the ball disappeared over the wall into other people's gardens. It was also the reason why there was no kicking allowed in rugby and no ball was allowed to go over shoulder-height in soccer. Looking back, there seemed only two ways that a game could ever end: when darkness fell or when the ball did finally go over a garden wall and the son of the house did not play for either side. We would then wander disconsolately home. The wonder of it all is that I can never quite remember when it finally came to an end. I can never pinpoint the year or the age when it stopped. It was as if I woke up one morning and in retrospect realised that it had ended some time ago. All that I do

31

remember is that they were invariably exciting games,
encompassing in miniature the thrills of what I imagined
actual matches to be. The Saturday morning of a rugby
International or the Cup Final usually meant that we
played out the game beforehand. Whether it was a couple
or a dozen of us we would devise a method of playing the
game; it was all haphazard but inventive. There was no
adult to dictate terms, the child's imagination ruled. There
were no restrictions except by common agreement. We ran
and played at will. Emphasis was on flair and the
unorthodox, on an individual's talent – talent full of flamboyant gestures. Looking back, I remember the joy of
skilful display in beating a man, hoping that there was
another to beat, of performing a successful trick time and
time again and perhaps failing sometimes in the attempt. It
was not arrogance, it was simply pleasure in my own
physical ability and in doing something well. The trick was
outwitting, out-thinking an opponent, using guile and
technique, skill and timing, not power and brute strength.

In soccer, if you saved a goal you did so in the
exaggerated fashion you thought Bert Trautmann or Bert
Williams did; if you played at outside right you imagined
you did it with the grace of a Stanley Matthews; if you
headed the ball you did so like Tommy Lawton or shot it
like Stan Mortensen. If you scored a half-century on the
tarmacadam roads you did it with the combined skill of
Worrell, Weekes and Walcott, or Denis Compton. And
after 1955, if I ran with the ball in my hands I did so with
my head tilted back like Cliff Morgan – if I played outside-
half, that is. If I played at centre or on the wing then I
would be a Butterfield or an O'Reilly. I did not have to be
a Welshman although I preferred to be one. It was the
essence of what I imagined their skill to be that I was
interested in. And when I say imagine, remember that TV
coverage was not what it is today. You relied on the written

word or a glimpse, perhaps, on the Pathé news. For apart from the occasional shopping expedition to Llanelli or Carmarthen, or we might venture as far as Swansea by train at Christmas, the other great treat was to go to the cinema and it is here that we watched the Pathé news. But more importantly we listened to the older people talk. The people in the village loved to talk, debate and argue on the only seat in the village, in the shadow of the church tower. Usually the subjects were politics or the garden and especially sport. Sometimes religion crept in, too. A child is fascinated by adult conversation and it was from these conversations, perhaps pretending not to listen in case they should suddenly become aware of me and the conversation falter, that I gleaned a lot of information about Morgan, Butterfield and O'Reilly.

1955, the year of my tenth birthday, seems to be a year that has stuck in my mind. Before that I am sure I was more interested in soccer; before that year I can remember the Cup Finals distinctly. I can remember collecting cards and pictures of soccer players and keeping a scrap book on them. Or I entered competitions where I had to recognise famous soccer faces behind a mask of shaving cream. The village boasted a soccer team and my step-brother, Delme, played. They had won the Darch Cup once. My father had played both games and had no real preference. Rugby gradually started making inroads, perhaps as a result of more and more of the children going to grammar school and being influenced by it. Rugby was the only game there, and the pupils started bringing the game back to the village. 1955, too, was the year of the famous Lions who managed to draw a Test series in South Africa. It was a tour that was evocatively described by Vivian Jenkins' book, *Lions Rampant*, and that book captured my imagination. From there on the round ball took second place in importance to the egg-shaped one

33

although I still played both. Those Lions set a standard that was to last until the 1970s. It was not only the fact that they had managed to level the series that was important to me but that they had done so with style and panache.

Saturday afternoon meant the smell of my mother's cooking – the smell of flour and green apples, the taste of jam tarts and Welsh cakes – as I listened to the crackling voice and anglicised tones of G. V. Wynne-Jones, 'Geevers' to his many followers, on the wireless commentating from Lansdowne Road or Murrayfield, Twickenham or the Arms Park. This was the time when the name McLaren was synonymous, not with rugby, but with racing cars from Silverstone. And the only guaranteed televised match was the one between Oxford and Cambridge on the second Tuesday in December. Again, it was left to the imagination to deal with the thrills of an international match.

Thereafter it was a long wait until Sunday, not necessarily for the written match report but more importantly and more influentially to listen to the village pundits voice their opinions on the game, all in Welsh of course – at that time the entire village had Welsh as its first language and a few of the older inhabitants could speak no other tongue. On those occasions there was very little need for me to be cajoled to go to morning chapel in Sion, because the majority of the male members of the congregation would inevitably remain outside afterwards to go through in detail the events of the Saturday afternoon match. Perhaps one or two of them had actually been there, so could give an eye-witness report. For an hour indoors I listened to the passionate oratory of the minister, then for an equal length of time outdoors I would listen to red-hot arguments over a Welshman's other religion. My own contribution was nil but I would gladly stand there, transfixed by this animated talk. I might fidget now and again, but I would want to give the impression of being unconcerned so as not to embarrass the adults. I did not want them to tone down their opinions because a child was amongst them; I wanted to be present to listen to the full heat of uncensored argument and I dared not leave until the whole subject had been thoroughly exhausted. Many a Sunday roast lunch I nearly missed as a result.

I did not necessarily want my father to be present at these Sunday debates, for I knew full well that I could hear his opinions on Monday evenings, when 'Evans the shoes', from Kidwelly, would come and collect his weekly payments on the shoes bought on HP. Once again the arguments would rage afresh. They were all the more fascinating because they did not repeat what could be recognised as the accepted *Western Mail* view. That paper, it was generally felt rightly or wrongly, had too much of a Cardiff and East Wales bias to it. We were West Wales and there was a difference, of course. I was much too young to discuss things with my father so I had to wait for an adult to enter the house before the real talk began.

These talks were not limited to rugby: my father adored politics, and if ever a name was mentioned with reverence, it was Nye Bevan. Whilst my father could recognise the idiosyncrasies, the weaknesses, the strengths, the delicate balance between good and great sportsmen, and he could argue sensibly and objectively about them and vary his opinions according to form, not a cross word in any circumstances could be said against the miners' favourite politician. In our house this man seemed to be beyond criticism. There was none of the cynicism that is so often attached these days to comments about politicians. Quite simply, Aneurin Bevan was idolised.

I valued these discussions so much that I would forsake everything to listen to them. I did keep my fingers crossed, however, that Evans would not call at our house until the weekly episode of 'SOS Galw Gari Tryfan' was over on the wireless. Gari Tryfan was a John Buchan-type hero, who pursued amazing adventures to keep the Welsh hills free of strange and evil goings-on and contested almost single-handedly with super villians from foreign lands. In the time-honoured tradition of these serials, you were left in cliff-hanging suspense at the end of each episode. This was the only concession I would make, hoping that perhaps they would discuss politics first, which I must confess did not much interest me, except for the way my father talked of Nye Bevan. By the second cup of tea they would get down to the real matter – rugby – and I was back with them after Gari Tryfan's adventures were over for another week.

My main regret is not having seen the great Bleddyn Williams play. Interested as I have always been with the subtler choices of manoeuvre in beating a man with a swerve or a side-step, I would have loved to have seen one of the greatest side-steppers of all time perform his skills. People say that he rarely, if ever, had the opportunity of doing this at international level, yet he did so week in, week out for the Cardiff club. The only opportunity I might have had was to go and see his very last performance in his club colours. I had been invited to go to Cardiff by car with the only family in the village who supported a club other than Llanelli – the Griffiths. The father, John, was a university graduate and a headmaster and the three brothers in turn had followed in their father's footsteps and graduated from university, the three sons from Cardiff. So in their keenest years between 18 and 22 they had followed the 'blue and blacks'. Whilst everybody else in the village knew the Stradey players by heart and followed their fortunes through thick and thin, the Griffiths family held up the pride of Cardiff colours. Arguments raged, particularly after Sunday morning chapel. At no time was debate fiercer in our village than during the 'fifties, over the question as to who should play outside-half for Wales.

The Big Five were in no doubt, it seems: Cliff Morgan played twenty-nine times for Wales, Carwyn James only twice. But to every adult man in the village, it should have been the reverse. It was clearly Cardiff favouritism – but the Griffiths were safe in the knowledge that the Big Five at least were on their side. They were considered something close to fifth columnists in the Scarlet camp, but it did not matter to them that their favourite players were Morgan, Matthews, Judd, Willis and the rest. And of course Bleddyn. There was no need for a surname here. Indeed, the elder Griffiths boy, Geraint, named his son after him.

The Griffiths asked me to accompany them to pay a final homage to the great man. The large black Austin with its comforting smell of leather could take us all and I was prepared to go. Had they gone on time I would have seen it all but they were notorious for never leaving at the right time. There was no sense of urgency, always time for another cup of tea. So by the time they were ready to go, my parents had changed their minds and decided that Cardiff Arms Park with its expected capacity crowd was no place for a ten-year-old.

If my memory serves me rightly there was a strong feeling even then of having missed out on something important. Of course it was years later that I was to become aware of the significance, particularly since my side-stepping style has occasionally been likened to that of Bleddyn Williams. I wish I had been there. I was well into my teens before I eventually made my first trip to the Arms Park and I was fortunate enough then to see another legendary figure, Cliff Morgan. That I did not miss.

For me, like every other rugby player in the village, Saturday afternoon when the Scarlets were playing at home inevitably meant a journey to Stradey. Whilst there were many scarlet heroes, it was Carwyn James who stood out for me. There were those who admired his drop kicks, or his subtle, canny kicks to touch; I thrilled to his side-steps, his running with the ball. Years later, people do ask about my side-step and how to teach it. My simple advice has always been to go and see a player do it and then to try and imitate the pattern. I have yet to see somebody teach it successfully. Breaking down the movements into simple steps and gestures has always seemed to me to be awkward and cumbersome and very mechanical. I believe in something that Cliff Morgan once wrote: 'You can always teach someone *how* to do things but never *when*. The secret of success is timing – in work, in sport and in enjoyment.' I may not have seen the great Bleddyn do it but I did see Cliff Morgan's adversary for the Welsh outside-half position, Carwyn James, and he was a master par excellence at eluding people in this way. He teased opponents, almost daring them to tackle him, persuading them to go one way when he had made up his mind to go the other. By many people's standards the measurement of a player's contribution to a game is in direct proportion to the amount of mud he has managed to accumulate on his kit. For Carwyn the reverse was true; he hardly needed to shower at the end of a triumphant game.

So in those early years my rugby interest was developed by listening to the way people talked about it and from the improvised games we had in the streets. These games were not the only diversion. Hermetically sealed as the village seemed to be from outside influences, we as children did much as we wished. There was open space all around, the fields and woods were a constant source of entertainment and the sea and the sand down below were a haven in the summer. We made primitive dens, or camps out of branches and the undergrowth, bows and arrows were made from saplings and thereafter we would hold target competitions or act out the roles of our swashbuckling heroes of the silver screen like Errol Flynn or Burt Lancaster. A child's mind a kingdom is and on a Saturday a child could be on the winning side against England in a rugby International and by the late afternoon he could have saved a maiden in distress from the clutches of an evil baron. All the sweat and dirt accumulated by the late evening could be washed away with a swim in the sea.

All this may seem a rather rosy view of my childhood, an over-simplification or even an idealistic way of looking at my own past. But it is the way I remember it, or perhaps the way I choose to remember it. Was it really like this? I must admit that memory does play tricks, that it has a favourite habit of allowing one to remember only the good points. Did the sun always shine in those summers? Did we really do all those things? Were there enough hours in the day? I doubt it. There were rainy days that no doubt kept us indoors playing Monopoly, long days of boredom and frustration, twiddling our thumbs, wondering what to do. There must have been farmers who sent us away from their fields and woods, parents who moaned and were angry. Bickering and jealousies, too, among the children. But I cannot really remember in detail those times. I can remember that on a clear day you could see the four old counties that bordered the three landward sides of Carmarthenshire and that to the south you could just make out the shape of Lundy Island. It was a magical looking island, hazy and indistinct. To us children it epitomised the attraction of the outside world, and it figured largely in our games of fantasy as Avalon, Napoleon's Elba or the Isle of Monte-Cristo. Just as Edmund Dantès in the latter story had to leave the island which had enriched him, so the time would come when I, too, would have to leave the village.

3

Of course childhood was not all play and a gradual awakening of interest in rugby football. There was school to attend and the primary school was within walking distance of my house. There were no organised games, no physical education at Llansaint Primary School. There was no need to introduce into a formal structure something that children in a rural community could get quite easily without guidance outside school hours. In any case the facilities were just not available, not even a hall. The school and its staff had different priorities. There was plenty of reading, writing and arithmetic with some light relief in the form of music, poetry and history. The aim of the education we had there was to get us through the eleven-plus exams and the school had a high percentage of passes to the Grammar School in Carmarthen. For almost everybody in the vicinity this school was known as the 'Gram', even though there were several grammar schools in the area. Because it was the oldest, and to the resentment and displeasure of Whitland, Llanelli and the others, the 'Gram' quite simply meant the one in Carmarthen.

In 1957 I went to Queen Elizabeth Grammar School, Carmarthen, and for the next six years the routine was the same: at 8.15 am an Eynon's bus came to take us to Carmarthen and the same bus brought us back at 4.30 pm in the afternoon. It seemed an awesome prospect to begin with. The school was ten miles away, and for a twelve-year-old brought up in a close community it seemed a very long way away indeed. The school has a very great tradition (it recently celebrated its four hundredth year, having started way back in 1576), and its old, grey stone buildings had a forbidding look to a timid new boy.

The insistence on school uniform also represented a formality to which I had not been accustomed. Wearing the school cap, for instance, was absolutely essential at all times and if you were caught not wearing it coming in or out of school you could be punished. Like most other schools, probably, it was this particular rule that caused the greatest objection. Those were the days in the mid-fifties of the Brylcreem, Tony Curtis hairstyle. Caps would therefore be balanced precariously at the back of the head in order that the coiffure at the front should remain unruffled. The boys' and the girls' Grammar School, although adjacent, were segregated halfway up the long drive and the vainer lads went to great lengths to make only a gesture of wearing the cap.

For a boy of twelve with very little interest, at least at this stage, in attracting the attention of the opposite sex, the main fear on that first day was the initiation ceremony for all new boys. Stories had filtered back to the village of how all the new boys received a 'ducking'. This meant that your head was held under a tap of cold water. It might be worse in that you could be stripped to the waist and given a thorough wetting. Worse still, or so the story went at the time, a whole crowd of senior boys could get hold of you and you might be up-ended, taken to the lavatories and be held suspended over the toilet while somebody pulled the chain. For all my trepidation this did not happen to me and I am still not sure whether it happened at all to anyone.

Education at the school was strict and formal and it had

41

a reputation of high academic excellence, but the physical education teacher, Bill Stanton, had very few worthwhile facilities at his disposal – a gym, a rugby pitch and one tennis court was all he had to cater for the five hundred or so pupils. It is often said that it is better to have inadequate facilities and a good teacher than to have good facilities and an inadequate teacher. The truth of this axiom could easily be seen at Queen Elizabeth Grammar School in those years. Such limited facilities extended Bill Stanton's ingenuity to the limit – increased his frustration, too, I would say. Through necessity, not choice, it was a limited programme of activity which he had to offer.

Fortunately rugby was my main interest and that was played throughout the winter months, provided that the pitch was not waterlogged. This grassed area was transformed into an athletics track and cricket square in the summer months. Not at any time did I question the fact that there were so few facilities and so little variety in the timetable: I accepted it as being in the nature of things. The same applied, I assumed, to countless other schools the length and breadth of the country. At least the school satisfied my choice of sport but I have wondered since then what might have happened to those less inclined to rugby than I was. Who in our school knew anything of badminton, squash, volleyball or any of the other countless attractions that there are today? If the weather was too wet for games, we went on a cross-country run or we had potted sport indoors. Nothing of the sort would be tolerated today and quite rightly, too.

As far as rugby was concerned, coaching as we know it today was practically non-existent. We may have practised passing and kicking but certainly there was no discussion of the technicalities or the minutiae of the game. If the weather was wet and the field heavy then it would be a forward struggle, if the weather was fine and the field firm then there was the chance of a running game. It was almost as simple as that.

There were inter-form matches after school but there were no regularly organised matches against other schools until you were fourteen years of age. At that age, too, you first prepared for regular weekly matches if you were picked for the Carmarthen and District XV, which was formed from schools in the area and played against similar teams from other areas. Fixtures were planned in advance and you knew exactly who you would play against throughout the season. It was all organised by the Welsh Schools Under-15 Association, in which Glyn Davies, Neil Davies and Brynmor Roberts played an important role. It was at this stage that I first encountered area trials for the Welsh team which meant that if you were good enough and successful enough you could go on to represent Wales for the under-15 age group. When the time came I was selected for the West Wales area trial but got no further. I would like to think that I had the skill but I most certainly did not qualify in size, and physical stature seemed to play an important part in selection. I did learn very early on from reading the *Carmarthen Journal* what the word 'diminutive' meant: if ever I scored and deserved some mention, that adjective often turned up as a description of the scorer.

In the area trial I played at centre on a wet and soggy pitch. My opposite number was Terry Price, who later played for Wales at senior level at full-back. He seemed an enormous boy for his age. As far as I can remember, neither of us did much during the game to prove which one of us was the better centre (thanks more to the weather than anything else), so it was he who went forward to the next trial. He was a brilliant rugby player and I did not begrudge him his place. To be quite frank, I had no burning ambition at that stage to play for Wales under-15 group. I readily accepted that I was not quite big enough and the way I felt was that if it happened to come my way, well, that was a bonus.

But Ryland Marks, a friend of mine from the village, played at outside-half for the same district XV and in the same area trial. He did succeed in going through to the next trial, and the next, and the one after that, until one morning he was told he was going to play for Wales against England at Twickenham. Now that to me was something to ponder on. For the first time it suddenly dawned on me that it was possible after all for the likes of me, living in a sheltered village like Llansaint, to achieve such a goal. It had always seemed that such things only happened to other people who lived in big towns elsewhere, to be read about in newspapers and to be admired and envied from afar. When Ryland Marks brought his red velvet cap and red jersey with three feathers on the breast back to the village it was something to wonder at. But more, much more than that, it strengthened my own resolve to play for Wales. If Ryland could do it then so could I. Of course I had always dreamt of playing rugby for Wales but it had always been no more than a dream. Now it had a basis in reality; it was after all something which could be achieved, something no longer to dream about but to be aimed for.

Fortunately, the second chance would come to me two years later, a chance to go for a secondary school cap at under-18 or under-19 level; there were no national teams at the under-16 or under-17 stage. With 'O' levels over and during my first year in the sixth form, my PE teacher, Bill Stanton, advised me that it might be worth doing some weight training: it could help my sprinting in athletics and it would help to fill me out a bit. So in lunchtimes I did precisely that, making what I could of the facilities available. It was at this time, too, that I started to train on my own at home. I went out in the evenings on cross-country runs or did some road running. This was a conscious decision on my part, that if I was to succeed then I had to get fitter. The improvised games in the village had come to an end a long time ago, so I had to make up for this loss.

There were training sessions after school hours and these usually took the form of the first XV playing against the second XV or a mixture of the two. I would catch a late bus back to Kidwelly and walk the rest, a two-and-a-half mile hill climb back to the village. As I walked home in the dark and away from the bright lights, I had to pass three cemeteries and if anybody asks how it is I can run so fast, these places of rest have a lot to do with it. I would run past these, kit bag and all, as if a chariot of fire was after me. A strict Nonconformist upbringing, with its emphasis on fire and brimstone sermons, had put the fear of God into me.

In the summer I dabbled at sprinting in athletics but I never got on with this sport. I used to get so nervous before the start that I became physically sick. Such stress did not seem to me to be worth the effort and I simply did not enjoy it. Whilst I have always enjoyed running for its own sake, I have never enjoyed competing in it. Even much later, when a coach at the end of a training session would line everybody up on the try line for a few sharp sprints, I would always feel uncomfortable about it. I have never been able to explain this fully to myself as I can be totally committed and competitive on the rugby field. It may be that I am not by nature a very competitive person except in rugby football. Even nowadays when I play squash it is more important that the match should be enjoyable with exciting rallies than that I should win. Although of course I go out with the intention of winning I am not intensely competitive about it. Rugby probably satisfied my competitive urges. It may be, too, that I prefer to motivate myself by my own standards rather than by competing against others to be the first to reach a line or a tape. That way has always seemed to me to be artificial. People frequently ask me what my time is over a hundred metres and I answer that I honestly do not know. In any case I made up my mind in school that I would not take part in athletics: if I was to succeed then it was going to be at rugby football.

In the 1962–63 season I was captain of the school first XV and turning out for the odd game during the season with Kidwelly. To get to the Welsh Secondary Schools XV there was a long road to travel, through district trials, county trials, area trials before the Welsh trials proper began. We trialists had to travel to Llandeilo, Neath, Ammanford, Newport, Maesteg, Cardiff and in amongst this lot we were due to play against the Welsh Youth (our contemporaries in age who had left school early) and Yorkshire. The trials started before Christmas and the Internationals did not take place until March or April. The match against Yorkshire, for which I was not chosen, was to take place much earlier – just after Christmas, I think – although in the event it was snowed off. However enthusiastic one was, all these trials could become something of a burden and, with a Welsh jersey as the goal, this was one case where the maxim that it is better to travel hopefully than to arrive did not apply.

My exclusion from the Yorkshire match only served to whet my appetite and I trained throughout that notoriously cold winter of 1963. When the weather was too bad to go out, I did a rudimentary form of circuit training inside the house. Goodness knows what my parents made of that. Both of them by this time had taken an interest in my rugby and they followed me the length and breadth of South Wales for those trial matches. At first they had taken little notice of my rugby, except to worry that I might take too keen an interest in the game at the expense of my education.

But when I was about fourteen they accepted that it was a losing battle they were fighting and thereafter they actively encouraged me.

During this time I was playing at outside-half, as I had done since my year with the under-15 district side. Somewhere along the line, I think it was early on in a trial at Llandeilo, I was converted back to centre. It seemed that there were two of us with equal claims to the outside-half berth. One of us had to switch. A change of position was not to come my way again until six years later in 1969, when Clive Rowlands suggested to me in a plane coming from Christchurch to Auckland in New Zealand that I might like to play on the wing. Like the decision in 1963, that too had its merits!

In the event I represented Wales at centre against England at the Arms Park and at outside-half against France at Bergerac. After the excitement of being chosen to play against England, I had a scare: I badly twisted my ankle in the few days leading up to the International. Whilst I wondered whether I should play or not, I heard only dissenting voices around me, surprised that there should be any question over the matter. I thought of putting the problem before Rowley Jones, a senior selector at the time who later became Welsh Rugby Union President, but I was the only doubting Thomas – everybody else said I should and must play! Worrying about the injury almost overshadowed the greatness of the occasion, but in the event I took the field with a heavily strapped ankle. A few weeks later I took my first-ever flight out of the country to play France, the first of many that were to follow.

But what of the rest of my future, what career was I to follow? I had made up my mind about twelve months previously that I wanted to be a teacher and because Bill Stanton, the PE master, was a former Loughborough student, he persuaded me that I should follow him to that college for my tuition. Because of its reputation for producing fine athletes – in the broad sense of the term – I agreed. Loughborough it was.

1. Aged 3, with sisters Mair (left) and Elizabeth (right).

2. The village children, proud of their soccer team's victory in the Darch Cup. I have just scraped in at the left of the second row from the front, despite being nearly elbowed out – a pattern that was to be repeated in the future.

3. Captain of the Queen Elizabeth Grammar School, Carmarthen, rugby XV.

4. Captain of Cambridge in 1970. The team had a good record overall, but lost the Varsity match to an Oxford side which had had an undistinguished season up to then.

5. Scoring for London Welsh against Llanelli, Clive Rees in pursuit.

6. Playing in the Middlesex Sevens for London Welsh against Richmond. It is a pity that the same enjoyable competition cannot be repeated in Wales.

7. I'm over the try-line – now can I get nearer the posts? Scoring against Ireland at the Arms Park in 1971.

8. With some of the boys from Christ's Hospital in their distinctive garb.

9. On my way to the try-line for my first International try as a wing – against England at the Arms Park in 1971. It's a good job I don't look at myself when I'm running!

10. Scoring the Lions' first try in the vital Third Test against New Zealand at Wellington in 1971.

11. My father and mother, fiancée Cilla and the autographed ball from the Fourth Test at Auckland in 1971. Typically, Gareth Edwards stuffed this ball up his jersey when the final whistle went but kindly presented it to me in the dressing room afterwards.

12–13. The Irish connection. Left: the Gibson boy in motion, with mind and body in perfect unison. Below: looking at this photograph of Willie John McBride (with Fergus Slattery behind him) it is difficult to imagine his soft, lilting voice singing 'Danny Boy' or 'Scarlet Ribbons'.

14. A sight seen all too rarely, alas: David Duckham, a truly great player, on the attack in an English jersey.

4

By going to Loughborough I finally broke the umbilical cord that tied me to Llansaint. Little did I think, however, when I moved into my digs with Mrs Porter in Storer Road, that I had left home for good. Somehow, at the back of my mind, I always felt that I would return to Llansaint. A lot of people make a conscious decision to leave home to look for fresher fields but not me: perhaps naively, I felt that my three-year stint would only be an interlude, after which I would return. It only gradually dawned on me that the break from home had been made.

Two of us shared digs with Mrs Porter for two years. My partner was Istvan Komaromi, a Hungarian who with his parents had escaped from Budapest when the Russians moved in in 1956. He had been a pupil at Bryanston in Dorset. Both of us would have preferred at first to go into halls of residence, but we soon came to appreciate Mrs Porter very much indeed since she served us with ample and very nourishing food. This was something we desperately needed after the vigorous activity at the College. There were others, like my friends Grays Thomas and Ken Evans, who complained bitterly not only about the quality of the food in their digs but about the quantity as well. Istvan and I stayed at Mrs Porter's for two full years, and he proved to be an excellent companion with whom to share digs.

Istvan was quite clearly in a different league to all my previous companions. He was of a firm, independent frame of mind, he was well read and something of a radical in his views. There was nothing he liked more than to have discussions: he questioned everything and never accepted anything at face value. Probably because of his background and his experiences in the 'fifties, he was suspicious of the accepted and more orthodox viewpoints. We spent hours, sometimes late into the night, discussing various topics either of sporting interest or from current affairs. He was intelligent and provocative: he would sometimes take a stand on something which he did not actually believe in, just to continue the discussion. It struck me quite forcibly at the time how much more open, more questioning his mind was compared to mine. Whereas, for instance, I might come back from a lecture having digested the information and accepted it, Istvan would start a discussion over tea on the subject. He would not automatically accept things as they had been presented to us. It surprised me to think that I had come from a background which in itself was fairly radical, yet I was as reticent as if I believed that the holding of opinions was the prerogative of my elders only. It was an early and important lesson of student life.

If Istvan proved to be something of a refreshing influence among my own comtemporaries, more important still was the influence of John Robins, the rugby lecturer at the College. He was a quiet man, reticent almost to a fault, but he was devoted to the game of rugby football. Looking back on the development of coaching during recent years, I would go as far as to say that he was the first man in this country to think so deeply, so constructively about rugby: its techniques, its tactics and the full potential of the fifteen-a-side game. Not only to think about them but to try to put what he thought into practice. He had studied the game in depth and the whole range of its possibilities from the principles of scrummaging and lineout to the subtleties of manoeuvre in the threequarters. Coaching manuals have now been written covering comprehensively the infinite varieties of the game's possibilities, but I would say that John Robins was already largely familiar with those ideas. It may be that I believe this because he came into my rugby life at an impressionable stage, but certainly he approached the game with ideas and theories which I had not encountered so far. Remember that this was back in 1963, a year before Wales embarked on their ill-fated tour to South Africa from out of which disaster eventually emerged the Welsh Coaching Advisory Committee and the appointment of Ray Williams as coaching organiser; yet at Loughborough the coaching that was to become the vogue throughout the land in the late 'sixties and the 'seventies was already being practised.

Although John Robins was recognised by a small band of people – like the UAU in their coaching sessions at Lilleshall – he was unable because of his reserve and introverted nature to sell his ideas to a wider public. He still had a profound influence on all the rugby-playing students within the College. It was he who brought to my attention the phrase, 'People in this country play rugby to get fit; they don't get fit to play rugby.' It did indicate the general trend of thinking in the UK. His was in a sense a very 'professional' – to use an unsatisfactory word – approach, yet he brought a knowledge and expertise to a game which elsewhere was only being dabbled at.

Sadly, things have changed since those innocently experimental days of the early 'seventies, to a degree which John Robins, whose intentions for rugby were always of the best, could not have dreamed of. Since then coaching minds have been at work and new skills have been developed to cope with the changes in the Laws of the game. There is an often-quoted saying in rugby coaching circles which goes something like this: 'There is no such thing as over-coaching. It is either good coaching or bad coaching. Over-coaching is simply bad coaching.' The problem with such an axiom is that if it is repeated often enough people will automatically believe it without ever questioning its validity. In any discussion on the matter of over-coaching this axiom is repeated ad nauseam and people blindly accept it as a truism as if there was no answer to it.

The main contribution that coaching has made in this country is that it has awakened people to the realisation of patterns and combinations within the game and has also extended our knowledge of techniques. Before, teams relied basically on the individual expertise of some players and the instinctive play of others, but coaching brought an appreciation of method. Unless we are careful, though, the balance will change in the opposite direction. I believe that we in Britain are reaching now the stage in rugby that Edward De Bono writes about in his book, *Lateral Thinking*. It can be said perhaps that the rugby coaching manual 'exists to create patterns out of its surroundings. Once the patterns are formed it becomes possible to recognise them, to react to them, to use them. As the patterns are used they become more firmly established. The pattern-using system is a very efficient way of handling information. Once established, the patterns form a sort of code.' This is the stage we have reached now. He goes on to say that 'insight, creativity, and humour are so elusive because the mind is so efficient . . . Inseparable from the great usefulness of a patterning system are certain limitations. In such a system it is easy to combine patterns or to add to them but it is extremely difficult to restructure them . . . Insight and humour both involve the restructuring of patterns. Creativity also involves the restructuring but with more emphasis on the escape from restricting patterns . . . there is about creativity a mystique of talent and intangibles.'

This is the stage we are likely to reach next. Knowledge and technique are now becoming so accessible that we are apt to forget about individual talent. Is it an indication, perhaps, that as so many people complain about the lack of humour in the game, so there is the corresponding rise in violent behaviour? If we take the whole thing too seriously, may we not also lose insight and creativity? The essence of Welsh rugby, and indeed rugby as a game, allows for displays of imaginative daring which goes further than logic or any method should allow. It should allow for a further dimension of perception and imagination which encourages inventiveness instead of just simply patterns and drills which tend towards the mechanical.

An example of the increasing rigidity of thinking about the game is the emphasis on midfield manoeuvres to cross the gain line. Rather than improving skilful, quick passing to move the ball into space with the minimum of delay, the general rule is to cross the gain line close to the set piece. Such moves have in my opinion been worked to death. It seems to be ploys, ploys, ploys. Whereas crash balls, half-back scissors and the rest should be alternatives, they are now considered the general rule of play. The minds of players have been conditioned to think in terms of ploys, to use them constantly rather than as an occasional alternative. Whenever a ploy is used several players concentrate whole-heartedly on it, so they are unable to change their minds as the move is about to be employed or is under way without upsetting the whole manoeuvre. On the other hand, if there is no special move on, each individual player assesses the situation as it arises without upsetting the balance of the whole movement. He can afford the risk of doing something himself and the players around him can react accordingly. Using a ploy also tends to abrogate his individual responsibility, which is why I say it is a soft option.

It was curious, when I first took over the captaincy of Cardiff and played on the wing, how at every set piece the threequarter line would turn to me and ask what ploy or move was on. This may have been to show deference to me as captain, but I rather think it was more than that. They had grown accustomed to one person calling the shots. Unwittingly they were transferring their responsibilities on to me so that I made the decision for them. I preferred to pass the buck back to them and say, 'What do you think we should do?' I wanted each player to think for himself, to concentrate right throughout the game. It might be, for instance, that the centre might notice that the opposition's defence was weak in a certain aspect; then I would like to think that he would suggest to me that he would like to have a go at his opposite number. I wanted each player to be continually assessing the progress of the game and of his opposite number. The danger is that after the pre-match deliberations a player comes out with a pre-conceived idea of his opposition and of how he is going to play the game. Each player must be prepared to modify his ideas when he is on the field, but my fear is that coaches and players may become too entrenched with established ideas and ploys without attempting to explore other possibilities which are perhaps less simple to develop. Emphasis on winning only serves to reinforce this attitude: in order to explore the full potential of a team one must accept that mistakes will be made which in time may be eradicated.

The effect on the winger of the increasing dependence on ploys is to relegate him to a supporting role. He is no longer considered a creative player in his own right or as the first line of attack. There has been a gradual diminishing in importance not only of wingers but of centres too, and of the individual skills of passing, running at speed, swerving and side-stepping. I foresee a time when we will have to re-learn these skills. Nor has the winger's decline been helped by the development, particularly by scrum-halves, of the skill of kicking the rolling ball to touch. I am not so critical of this since when well done (and Gareth Edwards has developed it to a fine art), it can be an immense tactical weapon.

Another result of excessive coaching may be seen in the increasing emphasis in recent years on dominance at forward, probably as a result of our being considered inferior in this department to New Zealand and South Africa in the past. Quite rightly, during the late 'sixties and early 'seventies it was considered that we had to improve our forward play, thinking that a raising of standards in this department would cause the rest to fall into place. To a certain extent this has happened but I question whether the general standard of back play has kept pace; in fact, I believe that there has been a complacent attitude towards back play. Of course forward play is vital, but rugby is a fifteen-man game. No man should be neglected and each department should be given its due consideration.

Not only have we in Britain begun to lose our direction and our vision in back play, it is sad to relate that the same thing is happening in France. At one stage, every country that played rugby had its own different style or brand of play. Nowhere was this more true than in the way France played the game. Theirs was such an ebullient, refreshing, bubbling sort of game that everyone admired it but could not possibly imitate it – it was as effervescent as their champagne. Looking at their rugby in recent years, I doubt whether this is still the case. Instead of our taking what was best in their game and incorporating it into ours, it seems that they have sacrificed their traditional style and have adopted a more stereotyped approach, similar to the British way of playing the game. Jean-Pierre Rives told me after the France v. Wales game in 1978 that he had become increasingly disillusioned by the way his own country was now playing. The joy, the fun had gone out of the game because there was more emphasis on forward play; the style, the great panache of their backs and forwards, for which they were traditionally famous and which was admired throughout the rugby world, was continually being downgraded. That was why, he said, he was so pleased to be invited to play for the Barbarians. At least in that team there could be a sense of adventure and he and Skrela could enjoy running in the open spaces rather than being conditioned to play a certain type of game. To my surprise, he went further and said that when France won the Grand Slam in 1977, whilst the papers were full of compliments there was a genuine dissatisfaction amongst the rugby-following public in France. Yes, he said, they had won but there was no glory in it, it had been achieved by dour and uncompromising rugby. Winning, it seems, was not enough in France, the public wanted it done in a certain style. They had the champagne of success but it no longer sparkled as of old. It had gone flat.

Perhaps the most pernicious effect of over-coaching can be seen at junior school level, where the individual player's brilliance may be subjugated to overall team-work. I am not denying the need for team-work, but it can be accentuated at a later stage whereas the development of individual skills needs to flourish as soon as possible. In displaying individual skill there is genuine satisfaction that the child can appreciate, in a way that he cannot fully appreciate a team effort. That kind of appreciation comes later as the mind develops. Hugh McIlvanney of the *Observer* once wrote in another context, 'Other teams thrill us and make us respect them. The Brazilians at their finest rather give us pleasure so natural and so deep as to be a vivid physical experience.' Whilst he may be saying this as an onlooker appreciating the flair and skill of the Brazilian soccer team, their vitality and exuberance, I believe that a child when playing a game feels that 'vivid physical experience' which is 'natural and deep'. And that comes from the sheer pleasure of performing skills.

Coaching by its very nature implies a certain discipline, and I question whether children at this stage need to be disciplined in this way. Is it not better that they should be allowed the free expression of their skills? Whilst I appreciate there are very good teachers who will offer the correct degree of guidance and understanding, there are those who will subject a child to an unnecessarily rigid pattern of coaching. I have heard of, and indeed have seen, teachers taking their children out for training practices after school, sometimes two or three times a week. I have heard teachers talk about getting these children to a very good stage of fitness. Do children of this age need a programme of fitness? Of course not – they are quite naturally fit.

Furthermore, coaching cannot take place in isolation; what is done on the practice field must be put into effective use in matches and to this end more and more matches are arranged. These become highly competitive, and I doubt very much whether too many matches or too many competitions are a good thing.

It may seem that I have a bee in my bonnet about this and I certainly have. It is born out of experience in New Zealand. In 1971, quite a large number of New Zealanders were highly critical about the amount of rugby being played in their country at too early an age. At eight or nine years of age children would be involved in highly competitive matches; by the age of eighteen they would have gone repeatedly through the whole gamut of limited options available in a training session. The inevitable result was a large number of drop-outs from the game, saying that they had had too much of rugby football and wanted to explore other games that offered new experiences. The danger is

57

that we might reach a similar situation a few years hence. Too much organised rugby, especially competitive matches, at too young an age can also arouse strong emotions and bitter criticisms from the teachers and parents who follow the matches intensely. I have noticed that there is a lot of shouting and sometimes even abuse coming from the touchline. The child, instead of enjoying a game, enjoying the thrills and excitement, is inhibited by this kind of aggressive following. His pleasure in playing the game becomes secondary to the teachers' and parents' attempts to live their pleasures and enjoy vicarious triumph through a child. Listening from the touchline, I have heard supporters of school matches shout 'Smash him, smash him' or, far worse, to a boy about to tackle some boy 'Kill him, kill him'. Do the supporters realise what they are in fact saying? This may sound pernickety and of trifling importance, but I regard such a violent use of language as obscene. It is an easy way of bringing a sense of disillusion to the child, a sense of hostility which might ultimately lead to his withdrawal from the sport. Even if he continues to play, it will not be with the correct competitive approach or with a healthy and generous regard for the opposition.

★   ★   ★

The days at Loughborough were full of activity. Apart from the lectures, there were practical sessions in athletics, soccer, swimming, gymnastics and so on, so that by the time of our rugby training in the evening, I had already done my fair share of physical activity. Some of these practical sessions were in themselves quite exhausting. In athletics, for instance, it was not a matter of just accepting the theories of fartlek (jogging interspersed with patches of fast striding) or paar lauf (a sort of cross-country running) – we had to go out and experience them. In swimming we were training for the survival swimming medal award. Anyone who has done any of these activities will know how arduous they can be. Sometimes at Loughborough the one activity might be directly followed by the other; occasionally three or four activities came one on top of another.

On a couple of nights a week we would be recalled from digs and halls of residence in various parts of Loughborough to take part in a rugby session in the Victoria Hall (Vicky Hall). This was a large, hangar-type hall, bare of all apparatus. The call to the Vicky Hall for a session was enough to send shudders of anxiety, almost of fear, down my back, for once inside it was two hours of fitness training. Towards the end of the session you just hoped you lungs and muscles would hold out, and there were pools of sweat dotted everywhere around the hall. But taken with the gymnastics, swimming and everything else, all this did set a standard of general fitness for all time: I doubt very much whether I have been as fit again, even on the long tours. If Loughborough Colleges were going to gain some sort of parity with the older, more mature first-class clubs on the fixture list then it was essential that we should be fitter than they were. What we were going to lose in bulk and experience we were going to try to make up for in sheer fitness. To a large extent this worked, but not always. I do not believe there can be any substitute for experience, skill and know-how – a wizened few in the pack and a crafty pair of half-backs can slow a game down to suit themselves.

More important to me was the adventurous play that Loughborough favoured, although it was not a carefree kind of football. There was always a sense of purpose to every game – we were after all out there to win matches, as that is the purpose of the exercise. But the game was designed to use fifteen players and all manner of ploys and permutations were encouraged and used.

There was also the fact that the fixtures were nicely balanced. Usually we played university fixtures in mid-week and more often than not a first-class fixture on Saturday. Whereas we got too full a sense of our own importance against university teams, we were brought down to earth on Saturday when we played the midland teams or we travelled down to Wales. If we became slightly arrogant in our approach in the mid-week matches, John Robins soon knocked it out of us. A mere look from underneath those bushy eyebrows was enough. He taught us to respect the opposition and, if there was any sign of slacking off after scoring a lot of points, he would say it was important to keep playing at our best. To toy with the opposition showed a lack of respect. To add spice to our university fixtures we took part in the UAU competition.

The reader will already have gathered how great an influence John Robins exercised on my rugby career. Up until the age of eighteen I had largely developed of my own accord; I had picked up a little information here, gleaned a little knowledge there, gone to Stradey to watch the Scarlets play and listened to the people talk. John Robins came along at the right time, a time when I needed guidance. He advised and encouraged me to continue with weight training, and the facilities for this were far more extensive in Loughborough than they had been in Carmarthen. But he also explained why it was important for a relatively small man like myself to continue with weight training: in a game which caters for all sizes and all weights it was vital for me to be able to survive bodily contact with bigger men. Quite simply I needed to be stronger. A man may be tall or he may be heavy, but he may not necessarily be strong in relation to these factors. It is the ratio of body size and weight against strength that is of vital importance.

He emphasised, too, that strengthening my legs could help my speed. So in the summer months, when to the displeasure of some college tutors I did not take part in any competitive athletics, I continued with my weight training programme.

It was John Robins, too, who after a particularly casual game on my part which left me feeling despondent and cross with myself, advised: 'You set your own standards. You should always make sure you come up to them. Regardless of what people say, you know yourself whether you have played badly or not.' That is why it always seemed to me futile to tell somebody off for playing badly. He knows in himself how things have gone. What a player needs in that case is advice and encouragement.

The three years at Loughborough seem to merge into one. It was the time of the Liverpool sound, of the Beatles, the Searchers, Gerry and the Pacemakers and the outrageous Rolling Stones. Bob Dylan sang, 'The times they are a-changing' and times were indeed changing. The period had started with Macmillan as Prime Minister and saw the rise of Harold Wilson as Premier; Jim Callaghan was then Chancellor of the Exchequer. For me, 1966 was the important year because it was then that I travelled three times down to Wales to play in the Welsh trial matches (those were the days when it was considered necessary to hold three trials as opposed to the one to which we are accustomed these days). I succeeded in becoming reserve for the Welsh team in all four of the Internationals but got no further than that. It was also the year of the 1966 Lions tour to New Zealand, coached by John Robins. I remember listening in my lonely room, as I prepared for my final exams, to a bulletin which said that the Lions team had been chosen and that there was one uncapped player to tour New Zealand. I must admit that my heart did flutter a bit, thinking that perhaps from what the papers had said that I was the one to go. In the event, however, it was Delme Thomas from Llanelli, who until then had not played for Wales, who travelled to New Zealand with the Lions.

In 1964 Loughborough against all the odds had beaten London Scottish in the final of the Middlesex Sevens at Twickenham and as a result had been invited up to participate in the Gala Sevens the following year. It was in the final of that particular competition in the Border Sevens that Loughborough managed to beat Cardiff, who were also a guest team. There were two of us in the Loughborough team of that year who hailed from Wales, Geoff Davies of Llanelli being the other. As two very hard-up students we were unsure how we were going to make our way back to Wales. In the previous night's celebration we had both got to know the Cardiff players and committee, and as a result of an invitation by Haydn Wilkins, the Cardiff committee man, we both decided for company's sake to join them on the train journey back. By the time the train arrived back at Cardiff station I had made up my mind I was going to join Cardiff in the following season.

Since my final year at school I had played for Llanelli RFC on odd occasions during the vacation. In fact I had been asked to play for them against the 1963 All Blacks, on the wing. But I felt strongly that if I could not be chosen in what I then considered to be my rightful position in the centre, I did not want to be chosen at all. It would have been an awesome enough experience to play against Whineray's team and in no way would I wish to shoulder such a responsibility out of my accustomed position. In any case it was a point of principle on my part: why should I deny a place to somebody who played regularly for Llanelli on the wing? Fair enough if I was considered a better centre, I would have proved it, but to pick me on the wing not knowing what I was going to be like seemed unfair on the other one. So I declined the offer and in the event Terry Price, my former adversary at under-15 level, accepted the position.

Llanelli at the time seemed to me to be a little disorganised. There were times when I would turn up for a game, not knowing until I reached the dressing room exactly who would be playing. There seemed to be a constant stream of unfamiliar faces. For all I know I may have seemed to somebody else an unfamiliar and strange face. It all means the same thing: that it appeared to be a collection of individuals who went out onto the field to represent the Scarlets. The disparate elements did not quite make up a team in the fullest sense. I had come to expect something different from a team that I had followed right throughout my school days and had watched with excitement and admiration from the stands. The climax, or should I say the nadir, came when Llanelli went up to meet Harlequins in London and were soundly trounced by fifty points at Twickenham. This was an ignominious defeat and can mostly be put down to the fact that the team lacked cohesion and team spirit. In itself this was not surprising as the team had only been finalised on the platform at Llanelli station as we left that morning. After that particular result I made up my mind that I wanted to move.

How things have changed in Stradey when you consider the force that the Scarlets have been in recent years! The team with all its familiar faces, all its talents, has been an influential part of the rugby scene in Britain in the 'seventies in a way that would not have been possible given the seeming disarray that was common in the early and mid-sixties.

Another reason for wanting a move was that I liked the idea that a club should run two sides. Llanelli only catered for the first XV and if you were not in the first XV you would have to return to one of the many second-class

63

sides in the districts. You must bear in mind that there were no squads at this time. With Cardiff, blessed as they are with a second-string XV, the Rags, you could always be sure that if you did not get into the first XV a watchful eye could be kept on you and this would allow for continuity and progression. Allowing for the vagaries of selection at Llanelli at this time, and for my own lack of self-assurance, how certain could I be of first-class rugby? How long would I have to languish in West Wales rugby? With due respect I had no desire to play at that standard. I wanted to be certain of first-class rugby and it seemed to me that with two sides in Cardiff and about forty names in the club I had a better chance of achieving this at the Arms Park. It seemed a sensible decision, even though I came in for some criticism. Wasn't I born in the Llanelli area? Hadn't I followed the Scarlets all my life? Had I no allegiance to Stradey? I was selfish enough to think that my own rugby career came first, and since I was now a student in the midlands with a new career in teaching in front of me, the decision was easier to make than if I had still been living and working in the Llanelli area. In any case I had not played enough games at Stradey to become totally associated with it. Somewhere along the line, too, I recall one appearance for Swansea against the RAF, but somehow or other nothing came of that.

And so it was halfway through the 1965–66 season, after the first term of my final year at Loughborough, that I joined Cardiff, initially to play during the Christmas and Easter holidays. Keith Rowlands was in his first year as captain of the club and the team had Billy Hullin at scrum-half, D. Ken Jones and Tony Williams in the centre, Maurice Richards and Keri Jones on the wings: a formidable back-line indeed. Roy Bish was beginning to gain prominence as a coach and, as well as looking after his college XV during the day, took care to organise things for the Cardiff club. Although they were one of the first clubs to use a coach, the Cardiff club have not allowed him the pre-eminence that he may enjoy in other clubs. Preferring as they do that the captain should be accorded his rightful place as the leader of the team, the club has been aware that giving too much authority to the coach sometimes inadvertently denies authority to the captain. I wholeheartedly agree.

5

At the end of my time at Loughborough I did consider emigrating. There were two forces tugging away at my mind. Before settling down to a teaching post in the UK I had a strong desire to travel, not drifting from one country to another but choosing a country to live in for a while; I felt it would broaden my outlook. On the other hand, I did want to play rugby for Wales. Whilst this was a great ambition on my part I did not want it to be a limiting factor in my overall view of life and its experiences. If I went home to Wales immediately it might become increasingly difficult to move away. The break, if it was going to come, would have to be made at the end of my college days.

Four or five of my colleagues, Istvan among them, were going to travel over-land all the way down to South Africa. Political controversy surrounding that country had not then manifested itself in the way that it has since. South Africa had many attractions: the climate was excellent, emphasis was very much on the outdoor life, there was a tremendous variety of wild life, salaries for teachers were better than in this country and of course rugby was a major game. All this sounded like an attractive and exciting adventure, yet there was the dilemma that the Welsh selectors certainly had their eyes on me. Then, during 1966 it was announced that Cardiff would be going on a three-week tour to South Africa the following summer. This seemed to me an excellent opportunity to see that country as well as giving me a year of Welsh rugby. In both senses I could see how the land was lying. With this in mind, I decided to find a teaching job and to see what would happen during that year. As it turned out, although I was not aware of it at the time, the Lions were due to go to South Africa a year later in 1968, and Wales to New Zealand in 1969, so it seemed that provided I could keep playing well enough my yen to travel could be satisfied. So it has turned out and the question of emigrating has never arisen since.

The year began in the autumn of 1966 with me taking up a teaching post at Mostyn High School, Cardiff, and with Keith Rowlands as captain of Cardiff club. By the middle of the season both these factors had changed: I had moved to a permanent teaching post at Llanrumney and Billy Hullin had taken over the captaincy from Keith Rowlands, who broke a leg which finished his rugby-playing career.

The injury had not occurred when Cardiff played the Australians before Christmas, and Keith was able to maintain the remarkable Cardiff record of never having lost to Australia. Little did I realise then that the next time Cardiff played that country I would be the club's captain and that the side would extend that unbeaten record still further. Keith Rowlands, a man with a fondness for words, gave a stirring pre-match talk when we got together for lunch at the Royal Hotel. It was the right mixture: lucid good sense about the tactics and the approach to the game, and plenty of emotion, too, recalling the tradition of Cardiff, what it meant to wear the blue and black jersey and what it meant to all of us to beat touring sides. It had a tremendous effect on me and I would like to think that what I had to say nine years later had a similar effect on my players. Keith gave us the feeling that there could only be one result for that afternoon's match, and so it turned out.

Cardiff won, but apart from the victory the only other thing that sticks in my mind was that it was the first and last time I took a 'crash ball' with any success. It was a move we had practised in preparation for this special match: within ten or fifteen yards of the line, with the scrum on the left-hand side of the pitch on our own strike, Billy Hullin would run wide to the open, make a dummy scissors with the outside-half and give a short ball to me on the burst. It worked well and I made the necessary half-break to give the ball to D. Ken Jones with a clear run to the posts. Although on that occasion it ensured a Cardiff victory, I must admit to a certain reluctance about being involved in such a move: it needs a big hefty centre to have any chance of success and since I lacked the size, I lacked also the confidence which is essential to any ploy – I was not made of such stern stuff. A few years later such block-busting ploys became commonplace, but at the expense of more subtle ploys. These moves should be moulded round a player, not vice versa as has been the tendency in recent years.

A few weeks after that Cardiff victory I was in a Canton pub with a few of my friends from Cardiff and Llansaint. Four of us had only just moved into a flat and, fresh out of college and organising our daily lives for the first time, we looked upon the flat purely as a place to eat and sleep. Certainly we had had no time to think of luxuries such as a television set, so it was down to the pub if there was some item we especially wanted to see – on this occasion the announcement of the Welsh team to play the Wallabies in the first International of the season. When Bleddyn Williams, who was chairing the sports programme we were watching, gave the news that I had been chosen to play for Wales, my friends felt that the best thing to do with the beer was to shower me with it – this was in no way meant to reflect on the quality of the beer!

Of course I was over the moon about it. But, as with all great expectations once they are realised, there was some sense of anticlimax. When the beer was thrown, the others in the pub looked round aghast at such adolescent pranks: they did not know who I was. The lack of recognition had a momentarily deflating effect and in retrospect the incident does reflect the changing attitudes to rugby players and how much more popular the game has become, even within Wales, in the last dozen years. Rugby players are now celebrities who appear on media chat shows and record programmes, while newspapers take up several column inches to give character portrayals of the players, and it has become fashionable for fashionable people to follow the game. LPs based on rugby have gone into the hit parade, cartoons about coarse rugby players have proved more popular than Andy Capp, and rugby-playing Groggs have emerged from John Hughes' gallery in Pontypridd.

The fact that I had been reserve for all four Internationals the previous year made me accustomed to the feel of such matches, and having played for Cardiff against Australia meant that I would not be over-awed by the big-match atmosphere: the time at Loughborough may have smoothed the edges of playing skill, but the training college grounds, or any of the other grounds that we played on, were after all no substitute for Cardiff Arms Park. I felt curiously at ease with it all when the time came.

Apart from it being my first cap and the fact that Wales lost, the match itself provides no lasting memory. The game was won by a very good Australian team and emphasised the achievement of Cardiff in their encounter with the touring side. That Australian touring party set a standard for all future Australian sides which not one has yet matched. To some extent, too, they made a mockery throughout the tour of the claims made in certain quarters at the time for the over-riding importance of good ball as opposed to bad ball from the forwards. Of course good ball is preferable, but the lack of it need not be an insurmountable problem. With the combined skills of a Catchpole at scrum-half and a Hawthorn at outside-half, however bad the ball they receive from their forwards, it can be turned into good ball for their centres and wings. There are checks and balances in the game of rugby football, and the wise coach is the one who recognises them and can put them to best use for the benefit of his team. Remember that this 1966 Australian team went on to beat the Barbarians as well.

At the end of the 1966–67 season, with five caps under my belt, I was naturally thrilled to have played throughout the season, but there was a sense of dissatisfaction, too. Somehow or other there was a lack of cohesion: yes, we all identified with Wales and recognised a common purpose to win the game, and each captain did his best to mould a team spirit. But there was no common strategy as such, no real direction or attempt to establish a style of play. Each player would do his best within a very loose framework but we were in effect a collection of individuals who went for a run-out the Friday afternoon before a game in an attempt to mould a team effort. We were like an orchestra or band which has all the notes but fails to put them into a pattern which makes music. We lacked a conductor – a coach. We always had a leading player as captain but there was a need also for him to have guidance.

A few years later, with the squad system in operation, we would play like a club team. We would spend a whole Sunday down at the Afan Lido, Aberavon, meeting at 10.30 am and finishing at 4.00 pm. On paper this sounds a good deal of training but in truth we would spend only about two-and-a-half hours altogether on the field, an hour and a half in the morning and an hour after lunch. The time off the training pitch, though, was just as valuable as the time spent on it. That was when we got to know each other, there were casual chats and jokes, perhaps we would discuss club matches or talk a little bit about tactics and styles of play. For the most part it was very informal and with the training it moulded a good team spirit.

In the event, during the summer of 1967 there were suggestions that the Welsh Rugby Union would nominate a coaching adviser, and indeed by the next season Wales had as national coaching organiser Ray Williams, whose influence on the game cannot be truly quantified. By that season, too, we had a coach for the national team. But there were troubled times ahead and the whole thing did not settle down easily. Wales arranged a tour to Argentina for the summer of 1968 and the designated coach, David Nash, was not invited to go. This caused a few rumblings and resignations on points of principle. It was as a result of all this that Clive Rowlands became national coach to the Welsh rugby team.

At the end of the 1966–67 season Cardiff embarked on their three-week visit to South Africa. In our company was Gareth Edwards. Even though he was at Cardiff College of Education, because of the College's policy he had not been allowed to play regularly for the senior club. He was none the less a member of the club and we embarked on the first of many tours together. Because Billy Hullin at scrum-half was captain, Gareth was bound to play second fiddle. This is not meant in any way to denigrate Billy Hullin's skill, for he was by any standard a very good scrum-half. His playing style, like his social style, was full of wit, with a penchant for the unorthodox.

We had barbecues – or braaivleis as they are called in South Africa – in Uppington, we sat round camp-fires and sang in Windhoek, we went wine tasting in Paarl Valley near Cape Town, we went big game hunting, we ascended Table Mountain, and we visited the renowned

Danie Craven at Stellenbosch University. In every sense it was an exciting adventure and both Gareth and I took a child-like pleasure in everything we did.

A lot later we no doubt became a little blasé about such things and ceased to look on in wide-eyed wonder. But then a lot later other things began to preoccupy us as Lions tours took on more importance: Test Matches in South Africa or New Zealand cannot possibly be compared in terms of pressure to Internationals in the home championship, still less to travelling on a casual club tour. It may not be necessary or desirable to travel the same route again, and in any case each tour has its own distinct flavour, but those early experiences of travelling overseas stood us in good stead for the tours, the successful tours, of the 1970s.

That tour to South Africa was for all of us an immense success. As time passes all tours, for a variety of reasons, have a special place in our memory. We remember a particular game, perhaps not only for the result but for the circumstances surrounding it; we remember a particularly gruelling training session or the after-match sing-song, a special trip or excursion or the humorous characters that were on tour. Tours are remembered usually for the good things and the happy moments. The losses are not entirely forgotten but are soon glossed over. The funny stories, the happy moments, are told and retold time and time again, be it in a quiet corner or boisterously at a bar in a great crowd. If the game was won, then the happier is the tale in the retelling.

For Gareth and myself that particular trip by Cardiff, our first tour abroad, holds a cherished and perhaps a sentimental place. The abiding memory from a time full of memories is the game against Eastern Province in Port Elizabeth – it is always that game which gives the context to any story about the tour, to identify the time and place. The joy of the tour was epitomised by the way we played in that match, and our performance is put into perspective by what went on beforehand: as soon as our bus left the hotel for the Boet Erasmus ground we started singing, and the team could boast of a fine choir-like singing (as John Reason, who followed the tour in preparation for the 1968 Lions, would no doubt testify), led by the manager and assistant manager, Haydn Wilkins and Lyn Williams. When we reached the ground the bus stopped but because the song had a couple of verses to go everyone, without prompting, sat still until it was all over. It was an emotional moment. When we eventually moved it was just like the game against Australia the previous autumn: there seemed only one possible outcome. Cardiff played a joyous brand of rugby (with Gareth, by the way, at full-back), so much so that even though it was only a club tour, without the extensive coverage that attends a major Lions tour, I was reminded of the game by a spectator in Cape Town in 1977. The impression the match made was as deep as that, and Gareth and I still quite often cast our minds back to it. It was, we thought, to set a standard. It had all happened so spontaneously. When we tried to repeat the atmosphere and perhaps reduce it to a formula again, as we did against Northern Transvaal in the last game of the tour, the magic was not to be repeated. In that game we were heavily out-gunned by those giants of the veldt. The moment was not to be recaptured, it was as elusive as trying to savour again a particularly happy dream.

*   *   *

During the summer of 1967 after the Cardiff tour was over, with no thought for breaks in training, breaks which were later on to become so essential, I carried on with my fitness training back home in Llansaint. I knew that New Zealand, under the captaincy of Brian Lochore and with Fred Allen as coach, were due for a short tour in these islands early in the following season before Christmas. I trained sometimes twice a day, two or three times a week. Maybe this was more than necessary but I was nervously conscious that I had to keep up the standards set while at college. Later on, in 1968, I remember saying to John Evans, now a reporter with BBC Wales, that I was very concerned about my level of fitness and wondered whether if I was to continue playing for Wales, I would find it difficult to maintain that standard which had been set at Loughborough. But I realised later that perhaps body fitness is very much like a reservoir: in the dry season in the summer the level drops a little but come winter all you need is to top it up. It is the same with fitness, and if I did not let it go down too far then it was a relatively easy matter to keep topping it up.

I was also aware that I did not want to be recognised for having played for Wales once, or for only one season. It was curious that at one stage I felt that playing for Wales just once would have been a wonderful feat in itself. Having done that, I did not want to be recognised as a 'one-cap wonder', which was in those days a fairly common breed. Having played more than once, I thought it would be nice to reach double figures. Allied to these thoughts was the knowledge that the Lions were going to South Africa later in 1968, and to be a Lion was another ambition. Would I not then be treading in the footsteps of that 1955 team?

Besides, I enjoyed going on those longish runs, particularly around Llansaint, whether it was in the fields or woods or on the roads. There were routes that I mapped out for myself. For the most part they would be enjoyable, but inevitably a time came during each run when I would need to apply some pressure, when I subjected myself to some painful short sprints with a limited recovery time.

There were longish strides uphill and alternating times of pressure followed by brief recovery periods: sprint the length between three sets of posts, for instance, walk one – that kind of thing. Always the pressure period came towards the end of the long-distance run when I was reaching the point of fatigue. This section I can safely say I did not particularly enjoy. I used to break up the days so that I would do this kind of thing in the morning and go out into Parc-y-Ty, the village field, or down to the beach in the early evening but I devoted most of my time to sprint training of a hundred to two hundred yards. Right at the very end I would do short, sharp, twenty-five or fifty yard sprints. My training has always been geared to this because in a game a threequarter needs his speed most over the first twenty-five or thirty yards.

I have never been sure what the villagers thought about this but at any rate I am grateful to my parents for allowing such an eccentric athlete to carry on in such a way. It must have seemed eccentric to people who had never thought of such things but the standard had been set and I was not going to let it slip.

In any case, except for the vigorous final section, running through the wonderful countryside around the village was an enjoyable experience. The Towy estuary is classically picturesque and from one side you can look across to Llanstephan, nestled among the surrounding countryside, with its imposing Norman castle. You can see the house where Lord Nelson brought Lady Emma Hamilton for his clandestine affair, and beyond the headland is Laugharne and Dylan Thomas's 'heron-priested shore'. Often I could have stopped to look at all this, to listen to the call of the curlews and the oyster-catchers, but to carry on running was a more urgent pressure.

Once the season started there was even less time for such dallying. Howard Norris was captain and I was nominated his vice-captain. My fellow-teachers and I were moving into a house and Barry John, who moved in with us, was joining Cardiff from Llanelli. Squad training was in vogue. As well as the ordinary Cardiff sessions and the Welsh squad there was an East Wales squad plus the Wednesday and Saturday matches. Friday night was the only night which was free. Squad training seemed to spread throughout Wales like a contagion. As a PE master during the day I was in my track suit and in the evening I wore it for training. The African violet colour of the Loughborough track suit was like a coat of paint: once it was on it was very difficult to find the opportunity to get it off. I would come home to tea in it and then I would be off with Barry John to some training session or other. It became rather frustrating, for all this rugby activity left very little time to do anything else; it became rather boring, too, as we seemed to be doing roughly the same workout over and over again.

Relishing as I do my own private time, enjoying my own company, I objected to a certain extent that I had so little time for myself. The Principal at Loughborough, Mr Hardy, had emphasised in his end-of-year speech to his parting third year that it was essential every so often, perhaps once a fortnight or once a month, to sit down quietly on one's own in order to take stock of one's situation and circumstances. It is possible to get so involved in something that in a sense you tend to lose direction; your time is taken up with so many things, so many details and commitments, that you lose sight of any purpose. In other words, you cannot see the wood for the trees. This was beginning to happen to me in the few hectic months leading up to Christmas in 1967. Rugby was such a dominating influence in my life that there did not seem to be any contrast between what I was doing in my career and what I was doing in my spare time; there was no variety to add spice or flavour to my daily routine.

I had vowed since leaving Loughborough and the influence of Istvan's more wide-ranging knowledge that I would read as much as I could, particularly novels. I read anything and everything from the most popular fiction to the most serious. Poetry and plays came within this ambit, too. But always at the back of my mind there were some niggling questions; like some particular troublesome sore, the more they itched, the more I scratched, the worse they got. To put it simply, why was it that one novel was more highly regarded than the next? Why was one considered a serious novel and another popular fiction? Why was one author held in high esteem while another one languished lower down the order? There were broad divisions and categories, fine distinctions and subtle nuances and I wanted to know why. I clearly needed and wanted some authoritative guidance.

During my first year in the teaching profession, when I had every intention of making it my career, it had dawned on me that in order to make any progress a degree was essential. Taking all these points into account, the one reason being no more or no less important than any other, I felt that a time spent at university would be the best answer. I had the constant encouragement of Jack O'Connell, my former headmaster from my first teaching job at Mostyn, with whom I had kept in touch and to whom I could always turn for advice, confident that it would never be less than sound.

There were one or two abortive enquiries about university entrance and it seemed that nothing would materialise. Billy Raybould, who was then at Cambridge, suggested that I should try Emmanuel College. He said that the Senior Tutor would be sympathetic and could consider an application if I would care to make one. I thought about this for some time before resolving that I should at least make an attempt. After all, I had nothing to lose. I decided to talk with the Senior Tutor, who turned out to be kind, amenable and very sympathetic. What I expected a Cambridge don to be like I am not sure – perhaps aloof, a patronising academic, unresponsive and coldly impassive. An academic D. H. Newsome, the Senior Tutor of Emmanuel, was, but none of the other qualities applied to him. The upshot was that he would in due course invite me up for a formal interview and said of course that he could not promise anything.

Meanwhile, training was well under way and preparations were being made for the Wales v. New Zealand clash at the Arms Park. This was to be my first encounter with the All Blacks but to my bitter disappointment I had to withdraw from the Welsh team shortly before the game with a niggling knee injury.

Ever since the days when my father talked about them I had held the All Blacks in awe. Any discussion about them was in hushed, almost reverential tones. From the way he talked they were indestructible. And from the way the 1967 team played they *seemed* indestructible; they were quite simply the best side I have ever played against. I made two appearances against them in four days – in an East Wales side that managed an honourable draw, and a Barbarians side which lost. Both results were achieved in the very dying moments of the matches. They had Meads, Nathan, Tremain and Lochore in the pack, Laidlaw, Kirton, Davies, McCrae, Steele, Dick and McCormick in the back division and were highly competitive, skilful and efficient. I learnt the same lesson in both games: they were not in fact indestructible but in order to be successful you must realise that the game is not won or lost until the final blast of the whistle. This may be a self-evident truth but in the heat of the match, when limbs are tired and aching, it is something that can be forgotten.

After Christmas the home Internationals started and preparations for the Lions tour got under way. David Brooks and Ronnie Dawson had already been chosen to form the management team. Traditionally the last match of the home championship used to be the Calcutta Cup match and it was on the following Sunday that the Lions team was to be announced. However, the announcement to the press was not made until the Monday. I was at school at the time, in the gym taking a lesson, when I was asked to go to the deputy headmaster's office as there was somebody on the telephone. It turned out to be Brian Hoey of BBC Wales and it was he who asked how it felt to be a Lion. If I remember correctly that is precisely how he put it. There was no preamble, no gradual lead-in, simply 'Gerald, how does it feel to be a Lion?'

I suppose I did finally go back to the gym and did go on to finish the lesson but I doubt very much whether I had my mind very firmly on what I was doing for the rest of the day. True, I had spent three weeks in South Africa the previous year and knew what to expect, but a three-week club tour is not to be compared to a three-month Lions tour. The emphasis is different, the pressures greater. A little while later a letter came, asking me up for an interview at Emmanuel College. By coincidence the interview was on the same day as the Lions' gathering at the Park Lane Hotel in London. The briefing and the kitting-out were scheduled for the afternoon, the interview in Cambridge for the morning. It was a tight programme but I did manage to keep to it, although I would not know until well into the tour whether I had been accepted for Cambridge or not.

The club season had not finished, but having been selected for the Lions I stopped playing. I simply did not want to risk an injury before the start of the tour. The 1967–68 club season had already had one further distinction, if it can be called that in the circumstances. Although I had captained the UAU on a couple of occasions, my first real opportunity to captain a team in Wales was with Cardiff during this season when Howard Norris was unavailable. The occasion proved to be a bitter affair indeed. It was against Neath at the Arms Park. Whilst relationships between the committee men of both clubs have been good, the same cannot be said of the players during this particular period. I am not certain why this should have been so, but in any case it turned out to be a torrid and ill-tempered game. The previous couple of encounters had been the same. Gareth Edwards has already gone on record as saying that he has only been frightened on the rugby field on two occasions, and this was one of them. So was I. The Cardiff committee men and the players were unanimous afterwards in calling off fixtures. It was a sad decision to make but the right one. This 'cooling off' period proved decisive and the two clubs have now resumed fixtures to the satisfaction of all parties.

Cutting off fixtures in this way is unsatisfactory but it is at least one way of curbing violent behaviour on the field. In recent seasons a great deal of attention and publicity has been focussed on the increase in violence not only in rugby football but in other sports as well. It is no simple matter. There are many factors involved and no one factor in isolation provides the answer to the problem. It must be said from the outset that the incidence of violence is minimal in comparison to the number of games played throughout the season but the general feeling is, and in some cases statistics collected do suggest, that the number sent off in a season is increasing. This may indicate not that violence is increasing but that referees are less hesitant in taking action in sending off.

Whatever the reason, violence in rugby is abhorrent and must be discouraged. Rugby is an aggressive, body-

15. Room-mate from Cardiff to Canterbury, Dublin to
Dunedin, Sydney to Suva . . .

16–18. Gareth's last try for Wales, against Scotland in 1978. This was a sight which became familiar at the Arms Park in the 1970s – a scrummage a few metres from the opposition line was an offer too good for Gareth to refuse.

19–20. Two great Welsh outside-halves. Above: whilst HRH Prince of Wales was a spectator during the Wales v. Ireland game of 1969, the 'King' played on. Right: Phil Bennett's eyes and mind are ever alert for attacking opportunities.

21. 'Sid' Dawes in decisive mood! I'm sorry, I didn't catch that – which way did you say?

22. The Welsh team, captained by Mervyn Davies, which played Scotland at the Arms Park in 1976, the first of the triple Triple Crown years.

23. JPR has caught a kick ahead, we have worked a scissors and now the opportunity is open for a counterattack as 'Benny' races back to support. Counterattack has always played a large part in John Dawes's approach to the game, whether with London Welsh or with Wales.

24. A hard, low dive gets me in close to the corner flag against Ireland in 1975.

25. Gareth never did like training, but this is ridiculous.

26. 'All rugby wingers should be born philosophers. Why else should they stand around for so long, waiting, as if for Godot, for something which may never come?'

contact game and quite simply there is no place in it for the person who plays without proper regard for the Laws. Moreover, every player should have due regard for both his opponent's well-being and for the spirit of the game – something which is constantly referred to in the Laws themselves. This means that in no way should there be any malevolent intention to cause serious injury to an opponent.

If I had considered the game dangerous I would not have continued playing but I did wonder at times what it was that motivated some players to trample or kick their opposite numbers. I once watched one of Cardiff's second-row forwards about to enter a ruck. Seeing the leg of an opposing player sticking out, he promptly started, from a standing position, to exert full body pressure on the leg. There was no purpose to the action except to cause injury to the player. In no way was he helping our side to gain possession and in no way did he know who the player was, as the remainder of his body was covered from view. As captain I felt it my duty to tell him that if I ever saw that happening again he would not be considered for selection. I reasoned with him that he could have done untold injury to the player, could indeed have damaged him for life. Also, he was not helping either himself or the team. And as a last appeal I mentioned that he could not possibly be doing it for intimidation, as he himself had no idea who the player was and certainly the player on the floor had no idea who was stamping on his leg.

Intimidation is expected as an aspect of the psychological competition between players and in one form or another is part and parcel of the forwards' game. But it does not last for very long in a match; it is a case of one player attempting very early on to gain the upper hand. Actions which are barely legal but are expected as part and parcel of the game will sometimes produce frustration and aggression but not usually. It is the unexpected, more often than not, that produces the flare-up.

When I refer to playing within the Laws, I refer mainly to playing within the Laws so as not to cause personal injury, but there is also a good deal that goes on that can be labelled 'gamesmanship' when a player does not abide by the Laws. By and large these are innocent transgressions but a continual infringement of, say, the law governing offside can lead to nasty incidents. It is up to the referee to penalise these infringements immediately. Otherwise the players tend to take the law into their own hands, and what was originally a minor incident can escalate into a major conflict, resulting in physical confrontation and violence.

Norman Sanson, the London Society referee, did take immediate action in the Wales v. Ireland game in 1977 when he warned the players after noticing a lineout infringement. When it next happened he sent two players off the field, one from either side. He came in for a lot of criticism which in my opinion was unjustified. He saw what was happening, gave a warning and as he was well within his rights to do, took the appropriate action in sending them off. Thereafter the game settled down without incident. Had he not done this he would have been seen as a weak referee and goodness knows what might then have happened. For a short while afterwards he seemed to be ostracised from the game and kept from refereeing top-level matches. Whether it was for this reason or not, he was refused permission by the French RFU to take charge of the France v. England game in the same season. It is no use at all if Unions issue edicts about taking measures to deal with violence, yet on the other hand they refuse to act in support of someone of Norman Sanson's calibre.

The 'spirit of the game' sounds these days old fashioned, almost Victorian in ethos, and is consequently looked upon with suspicion. But like it or not, it still applies. It is difficult to define precisely as it is in itself an imprecise concept. It has something to do with enjoying the game, recognising that it is a body-contact game, aggressive yet healthy conflict. It is a test of strength yet not violently so; it is a test of skill requiring cunning yet no deceit; it allows for tricks but not foul play; it can allow for roguish behaviour but not skulduggery; it is permissible to be called a rogue but not a thug; you can be wily and crafty but not a cheat. It is a game where an attitude of win at all costs would be the start of deterioration into tribal warfare; the thin dividing-line would disappear and allow the cheats and thugs to dominate; deceit and foul play would proliferate and skulduggery and violence would rule the day.

Whereas the responsibility for his conduct lies firmly with the player himself, the captain and coach can go a long way to instilling the right philosophy and attitudes. Training sessions are a time not only to practise skills and develop technique, but also to impart the correct approach and attitude. It is no easy matter to do this and it needs time to develop, but the responsibility of the coach and captain is much wider than is traditionally accepted. While the tactics, technique and skill are much discussed, how many give much thought to the transferring of the right attitudes? Feelings of aggression are instinctive, I am sure, but if given the appropriate environment they can be a learnt response, too. If overtly aggressive behaviour is reinforced during the long winter training sessions then it will overflow into the games, so the captain and coach should not try to build up feelings of hostility towards opponents.

How many captains and coaches, I wonder, give much thought to what they say in a pre-match briefing, and not only what they say but how they say it? These talks have an immense influence on a team, just as much as long hours spent training. The wrong approach at this time can arouse emotions and may result in a victory but whilst taking the accolades, the captain and coach must shoulder some of the responsibility if there are any flare-ups or violence. Some coaches may feel reluctant to condemn a violent act but it must be done.

I have mentioned the responsibility of the player and that of both the captain and the coach. The third factor is the club. Whilst the various Unions and the International Board can issue edicts, and they have a duty to support their referees, they are too far away from the point of action to be effective. A Union may, for instance, discipline the offender who has been sent off but the complaint is quite often made that the man sent off was retaliating. Since the clubs see the players week in, week out, it is they who are in a position to identify the regular offenders. However effective a player may be in other respects, and however his exclusion from the team may affect the performance of the team, the club's responsibility is to take action against the persistent trouble-maker.

I have already mentioned the part played by the referee. In the international arena, it is imperative to have neutral referees. Whilst this is common practice in the northern hemisphere, it is not so in South Africa, New Zealand and Australia. The referee who is neutral is more likely to be objective than a referee from the host country. The attitude of the visitors would be different, too, if there were neutral referees; it is inevitable that the visiting team will be tempted to accuse a referee of being biassed if he is from the home country. On the 1978 tour to Australia, the Welsh team and manager were placed in an invidious position of having a Test match refereed by a man from the very town in which the Test was played. Not only that, but he knew most of the Australian team well. It was very much like one of the home countries playing in Pontypool, Llanelli or Aberavon with ten local players in the Welsh team and a local referee. And the visitors having no say whatsoever in this choice.

The Welsh management protested but to no avail, even though I understand that it was written into the tour's agreement that there should be consultation. Not only was this unfair to Wales, it also proved embarrassing for the referee concerned. It was a unilateral decision and since the Australian Rugby Union stuck so rigidly to their choice, even when asked to make a choice of any other referee in Australia, questions were bound to be asked within the Welsh party as to why they were so inflexible. As a result the team went onto the field with mixed feelings about Australian integrity. Those feelings were most probably totally unjustified, but at least on other tours in the southern hemisphere a panel of three or four referees, from which the touring team could choose, was drawn up by the host country.

Neutral referees would do away with protests and arguments about biassed referees. Whether these referees are biassed is of course open to question; one does not like to question their integrity. None the less, there is this undercurrent of feeling when you tour overseas, knowing full well that in New Zealand you will have New Zealand referees, in South Africa South African referees, in Australia Australian referees. It is not a case, as is so often claimed, of sour grapes – a panel of neutral referees merely makes sound common sense and the game would be better for it. It might, although there is no guarantee of this, do away with the kind of violence that has disfigured recent tour matches. Most certainly it would do away with the kind of discussions that occurred in Australia in 1978. To have a referee say, as he did on one tour, 'It's not your ball, it's our ball' does not instil confidence in a player as to the objectivity of the referee's view of the game. It may have been said in the heat of the moment, a slip of the tongue, perhaps, but knowing the circumstances which surrounded the match, it could have only one meaning for the Welsh players: that the referee was clearly biassed. In Australia, as has happened in New Zealand and South Africa, there was acrimony beforehand, violence during the game and recriminations afterwards.

At any rate, it now seems that there can be no argument against neutral referees. Tours make enough of a financial profit to cater for neutral referees to travel. With neutral referees, at least both teams start equal in that whatever the interpretation the referee makes of the Laws, it applies to both sides. Such an exchange of referees can only be to the good, too, in that they themselves can benefit from visiting other countries. It will help them to appreciate and understand the problems. It is also argued that the referees in Europe improve by being subjected to inter-national match pressure every year in the home champion-ship, whereas in the southern hemisphere they rely to a large extent on tours.

It is perhaps in this area that the greatest responsibility of the various Unions and the International Board lies. These bodies are failing in their duty if they do not soon introduce neutral referees. Pressure at international level, particularly on tours, is such that it should not be further exacerbated by debate over the suitability of a referee. This added tension will only increase feelings of aggression and frustration which in turn can easily lead to violence in the game itself. I have gone on at length on this point: it may seem out of proportion to the size of a problem which is not immense in any case, nor do I wish to under-estimate the responsibility of clubs, coaches, captains and above all players themselves. But since there are signs that the problem is growing, now is the time to consider every way of stopping the violent element in the game. Clearly, it is a collective responsibility, with the major onus on the individual player, if the game is not to degenerate to the point where the proud boast of rugby people everywhere, that it is a game played by gentlemen of all classes, takes on a hollow ring.

6

The 1968 Lions tour to South Africa was a complete disappointment on the field to me personally. I had looked forward to it so much and wanted to establish myself as a Test player, but because of a couple of injuries a large part of the tour was lost. However good and enjoyable a tour is, it is never entirely satisfactory unless one plays regularly. If a player does get injured there is an almost desperate need to start playing and training again, so there is a tendency to rush things and perhaps to start training a week or so before one should – which only goes to aggravate the injury. I had an extremely troublesome ankle injury which gave me problems throughout the last two months. It might have cleared up had I given it enough time at the beginning to recover, but I was too impetuous and played in games from which I should have rested. At least I won my first Test cap, in the third Test at Cape Town, but when I felt that I would be making a bid for the final Test at Johannesburg, I dislocated my elbow against Orange Free State.

The tour was remarkable for two things. First, on the field of play there was a considerable difference between the standard of the provincial teams and that of the national side. Most of the provincial sides had very little to offer, whereas the South African team was an extremely efficient and powerful unit; no doubt both Syd Millar and

88

Willie John McBride reminded the 1974 Lions of this fact.

Secondly, off the field, I experienced the degrading face of apartheid. Whilst in Cape Town I had a telephone call from a student who had been a contemporary of mine at Loughborough. He was what they term in South Africa a Cape Coloured and had been at Loughborough on a one-year scholarship before returning to teach in Cape Town. When we spoke on the telephone I immediately invited him over to our hotel for a drink. He politely explained that he could not do that. So I, innocently, suggested that I go over to his place. This was also impossible, he said. Only then did the extreme perversity of South Africa's policy dawn on me. Here was a man with whom I had spent many an evening chatting over a beer at Loughborough, yet when it came to doing the same thing in his own country it was not possible. We met finally in the hotel garden.

Later on, when he took me around his school, my friend explained that he wanted, for the sake of his children mainly, to emigrate to Canada but he was not certain whether he would be allowed to do it. He was a well qualified teacher, he said, and he might have to stay in South Africa to teach the Coloured community. I never did manage to find out whether he went to Canada or not. There was something sharply depressing in the thought that this man wanted to improve himself, to get a better salary and standard of living, to use his qualifications fully, to teach with better facilities and, most importantly, to give his children a better start in life, yet he might be unable to do so because of the colour of his skin. The policy of apartheid may not be as simple and as straightforward as that, but here was a man who was suffering such indignity because of that policy. These thoughts were to come back to me in 1974.

Half-way through the tour in South Africa I received a

letter informing me that I had been accepted to go up to Cambridge University. In October 1968 I entered Emmanuel College for my first Michaelmas term. Initially I felt uneasy that rugby had played its part in gaining me my place. A lot later I was to push such thoughts to the back of my mind. If some of the students considered me to be in a privileged position because of my rugby, could I not look upon some of them as being equally privileged because of an accident of birth or because of the school that they went to? Anyway, here I was at Cambridge and I was going to take full advantage of it.

That first year was something of a struggle as I tried to settle down once more to the routine and discipline of study, combined with a lot of arduous training and regular Wednesday and Saturday matches up to the Varsity match, which Cambridge won, on the first Tuesday of December. Furthermore, after Christmas I was involved with the Welsh international matches and with the many squad sessions that were held during that season. During that eight-week Lent term I was away from Cambridge more often than I wished to be, too often for my own good. I was very rarely there at weekends. There was far too much travelling to and from Wales and it proved far too hectic. The traditional eight-week term disappeared in no time at all and at the end of it I was left wondering whether it was all worthwhile.

Later on, at the end of Wales' three-week tour to New Zealand in the summer of 1969, I came firmly to the opinion that nothing of the sort would happen the following year. I was after all in Cambridge to take advantage of the opportunities that had been given to me, to gain a degree and to get to grips with English literature. I wanted, too, since it was unlikely that the opportunity would occur again, to savour fully Cambridge student life and all that it had to offer. I wanted to be part of college life and I wanted to take my time to appreciate and do things rather than rush from one commitment to another. This I could never do if I was wandering up and down the land, training and playing rugby. And so for the 1969–70 season, when South Africa visited this country for a much publicised and highly disrupted tour, I decided to take a break from international rugby and made myself unavailable for selection for the Welsh XV. For the same reasons I also felt that it might be unwise to continue with Cardiff RFC. Quite naturally, up to Christmas I would be fully and totally committed to University rugby. After Christmas, however, though the fixtures in Cambridge continued, there were occasions when I could play for another first-class club. Being so close to London, it only made sense that I should join London Welsh.

In the second year, then, I settled down to a more definite routine of study than I had in my first year. There was a vast number of novels to read, plays and poetry to plough through. It was only when you sit down and consider it that you realise what a vast subject it all is. There was also a weekly essay to submit to the scrutiny of some tutor or other. In the Tripos there was a French paper to write, so I also attended classes in French with a fine, gentle lady called Madame Grillet, who must have had the patience of Job to contend with me because I was never any good and I considered time spent on French meant less time for English literature. Whilst I was not always very comfortable, for the most part I thoroughly enjoyed it and I shall be eternally indebted to Mr David Hay Newsome for having given me the opportunity to be there.

In my third and final year I did feel quite at home in the surroundings and I regretted very much how quickly the two previous years had gone. In that final year I was the captain of the University rugby team and for the first time I enjoyed the responsibility of being in total control.

Unlike other captains, who perhaps look on the team and the games to be played entirely as preparation for the one match against Oxford in December, I treated all the other games as important. When I came to think of it I felt that the teams we played before the Varsity match were harder and probably of a much higher standard than Oxford. We had to show respect for these sides if only to ensure that there would be continuity of fixtures for future years: it was insulting to consider Cardiff, Newport, Northampton, Coventry, the Harlequins, Bedford and the rest merely as a preparation for the one big match in December. For the most part we succeeded and beat most of them, including Fiji who toured this country during that year. Fiji had played the Barbarians at Gosforth the previous Saturday and had given them a thrashing; Cambridge on the Wednesday beat them.

The term was a successful one except in one vital respect – we lost against Oxford for the second year running. Peter Carroll, the captain of Oxford, had a completely different philosophy to mine. He had had a disastrous term with Oxford but, as he admitted afterwards, to beat Cambridge at Twickenham was the one and only purpose that he set himself. So it can be argued that my approach was wrong, and of course I was disappointed to lose the match, but looking on the term as a whole I could feel quite satisfied with our successes and with the brand of rugby we played. I used to meet Roger Shackleton, Phil Keith-Roach and perhaps Jacko Page in the Copper Kettle, a typically English tea-shop in Trumpington Street, at nine o'clock. They formed a little sub-committee to discuss the games and the selection of the teams to play. Although I retained the right to make the final choice, I wanted a consensus of opinion from these people before I selected the team. Then perhaps there would be a brief committee meeting with Dr Windsor Lewis and Dr Tony Craigen, both of whom have done so much to foster the game at Cambridge and for whom I have the highest regard. As soon as this was over I would wander past Corpus Christi and St Catharine's, down past Queens', over the Cam and so up towards Sidgwick Avenue for lectures. It was stimulating to listen perhaps to L. C. Knights lecturing on Coleridge or Raymond Williams discussing Hardy, to listen to George Steiner give not exactly a lecture but rather a performance on the subject of the Romantics. In the afternoon we would have rugby training, then it was time to drift back towards the college. Perhaps before arriving back at College a group of us would call in at Fitzwilliam, or 'Fitzbilly's' as it was commonly known amongst the students, to collect some cakes and go on to have tea in someone's room in another of the colleges.

By now it was 1970–71 and, having had a break the previous year, I had decided to resume playing international rugby in 1971. There was also the exciting prospect of a Lions tour to New Zealand.

When next I played for Wales at the Arms Park I was to do so on the wing rather than at centre. The decision had been made on the short tour in New Zealand the previous year. On a plane trip from Christchurch to Auckland Clive Rowlands, then coach to the Welsh XV, had asked whether I would mind playing on the wing in the second Test at Eden Park. Wales had taken three wingers and three centres on that tour and both Stuart Watkins and Alan Skirving were unfit to play on the wing, leaving only Maurice Richards. All three centres, John Dawes, Keith Jarrett and myself, were contesting for the two centre positions. Clive in his inimitable fashion was very persuasive. I was faster than both Keith and John, he said, and anyway this new touch-kicking dispensation law would give me far more opportunity to manoeuvre and to use my speed and side-step. 'You don't want to get involved with the heavy mob in midfield,' he said. 'We've got to use your genius on the wing.' Well, as someone else had said, there was no answer to that!

Looking back on it, there seemed to have been a gradual progression since my school days from outside-half to left centre, then to outside centre and finally to the wing. The next logical step was touch judge, genius or not! At the time, I must admit, I did not see it as a permanent job, merely that I would possibly see the end of the tour in that position. But both games, the Test in Auckland and the Test in Sydney against Australia, went very well. There was indeed more room out on the wing provided that the ball came out. Enjoying as I have always done the art of running with a ball, I found that the freedom to manoeuvre in the centre was being stifled and possibly discouraged. With the advent of the new dispensation law the backs were to a certain extent forced to move the ball rather than kick it. Fortunately for Wales this change coincided with the appearance of J. P. R. Williams at full-back, who is an adventurous runner himself. So not only did this dispensation law change the emphasis, but rapid movements to the open spaces seemed anyway an advantageous way for Wales to use the ball. There was plenty of running to be expected.

For the most part this has proved true, whether it has been for Wales, for London Welsh or latterly for Cardiff. The wing position is a terrific position to play, providing of course that the attitude is right in midfield. There are a great number of games when the wing does not see much, or occasionally any, of the ball if the run of the play does not go his way. A winger does not mind this too much as long as he is looked upon as a creative player in his own right and is given the opportunities when they do arise. An efficiency expert or consultant or whatever they are called these days could be forgiven for thinking that the position is superfluous in any real game of rugby football. For the most part rugby is full of hustle and bustle, to-ing and fro-ing, action and interaction. There is much foraging and contesting for the ball, plenty of tackling and body contact, yet a wing can play no part in all of this. There, just on the edge of the TV screen, just out of reach on the periphery of all that matters, is the number 14 or number 11, half moving, half checking. Will they, won't they pass the ball? Can he really be part of the same event? Standing in splendid isolation is a man who, for all that it seems to matter, could be out admiring the daisies or chatting idly to the mass of faces or passing his time in some other innocuous way. The wing seems to be wandering about a lot, glances frequently up at the threatening sky and, if he has a mind to, jogs up and down a bit on the spot in an attempt to justify the months' long training sessions. The occasional dog that strays onto the park seems to be taking more part in the game.

There is plenty of space out there and time to whistle several movements of a symphony if a winger is in the mould of a Mike Brearley, time to think on the meaning of things. John Ormond, poet and BBC Wales producer, once wrote to me of a game they were quite fond of playing in his local pub: to think up a rugby team selected from important historical characters – musicians, artists and so on. In suggesting a name for any position the reason for that particular choice should be given. For the wing positions Ginty Morris, a friend of his, came up with two philoso- phers: for the left side he produced Jean Jacques Rousseau (where else could he play with the initials J.J.?) and for the right wing Descartes (reason: 'I jink therefore I am'). It is no wonder that two philosophers were chosen, since all rugby wingers should be born philosophers. Why else should they devote so many long hours of training to their particular game, why suffer the pelting of the pitiless storm, why stand around for so long waiting for something to happen, waiting, as if for Godot, for something which may never come?

But I did enjoy playing on the wing for all that. It meant that I had to concentrate for much of the time when the ball did not come, that I had to anticipate a good deal and try to read the game as much as possible so that I could prepare myself for any eventuality. But more than anything what I liked was that the winger was the last link in the chain. There is a kind of responsibility for a winger to try and do something, to use his skills as much as possible and to manoeuvre into a good attacking position. Also, there was no room for making mistakes. The winger is very vulnerable in that he gets only a few opportunities and those opportunities he does get are usually in the wide open spaces of the field. If he makes a mess of things he has very little chance to recover, unlike a scrum-half or outside-half for instance, who is so close to the action and handles the ball so often during a game that if he does make a mistake he will have a chance to redeem himself later on.

The winger has always and will always be considered, I suspect, as the final link in the chain – the last line of attack – so he must not be found wanting in speed. Some wingers have been big in stature, some small; some have been elusive, others not; but what all top-class wingers have had in common is that they have been able to run quickly.

Size and elusiveness only very occasionally come in the same package: a big man is rarely elusive and vice versa. I always found it more difficult to play against the elusive runner because he can be so unpredictable provided that he can translate his thoughts into action with precision. Elusiveness needs quickness of thought and demands that the thought is quickly translated into action. But I am not saying that a player should flit around hither and thither in a haphazard fashion. He must be precise and accurate,

" I SEE GERALD'S BEEN OUT FOR A RUN.''

not bob and weave, stop and start. That could create confusion not only in the opposition, and not only in his team-mates supporting, but confusion also in his own mind so that he loses control of his own actions. In such cases too much is left to chance or to the lucky break.

The big man usually has fewer individual running skills and so his actions are more predictable. Playing against such a winger, I could align myself in such a way as to commit him to an action which he would find difficult to change. I could for instance position myself close to my own outside centre so that I approached my opposite number on his inside shoulder, thereby giving him the width of the field to run on the outside. I always felt confident of my own speed and that I could catch him. If not I would try to close up the gap between us so as not to give him time to lengthen his stride and build up steam, or to change his line of attack. Inevitably when I closed with him he would nestle the ball under one arm and try to hand me off with the other. This would effectively slow him down and, since I was never happy in carrying out the first-time tackle, I would wait for him to try a hand-off; then I could tap down his arm so that his shoulders would dip. Invariably he would hesitate and would falter and it was then that I would move in for a smother tackle, merely helping his own body weight to drop to the ground. The other benefit of such a tackle was that it denied him the opportunity of passing the ball to any other player coming up in support on the inside. I was often accused of being defensively weak because the action I have just described looked like hesitancy or lack of courage on my part. But for me it merely made sense: I was not entirely happy to commit myself to the first-time tackle, which needed a sure sense of timing, and if the timing was not right the opposite winger would be in full flight and I would not be able to recover.

If a big winger decides against running on the outside then the alternative is equally predictable. Knowing that he is big, he will put it to full use and try to run through you – a simple case of the shortest distance between two points is a straight line and an obstacle in the way is considered a nuisance. When this happened to me, I would stand in his way and take up the position advocated in the rugby manual – I would tackle him head on, take his weight and roll backwards. Sometimes I succeeded in bringing him down but if this failed I had halted his momentum enough to give time for my centres or the rest of the cover finally to bring him to the ground. Not at any stage in my career was I foolhardy enough to take up his challenge to try and match his strength with mine. That way madness lies. Compromise was a safer bet and I believe that it worked out rather well.

The disappointing feature about wing play is that very few wingers are considered as creative players in themselves. Other players in midfield are closer to the gain line and the modern preference seems to be to cross that line nearer to the set piece. Because of the risks involved, because of the lack of confidence in basic skills of running or handling, coaches are unwilling or unable to consider the wing as the man who should cross the gain line. This area of play has only been explored and tested by a very few people indeed: France did so in the 1950s and 1960s, the London Welsh and the British Lions did it in the late 1960s and early 1970s. A winger can be looked upon as a creative player in his own right and should be considered as a first avenue of attack.

With so many negative ideas about the creative role of the position, a winger finds that he has very little to do in a match. It would be a very foolish and misguided player who played a game for eighty minutes on a Saturday and trained regularly throughout the months merely for the sake of a few chance happenings on a Saturday afternoon. So there must be other objectives for a winger. One answer to this feeling of being out on a limb – no wonder he is called a wing – is to follow the ball and search for a piece of the action. It is an easy thing to say that a winger should go and look for the ball but if his side of the field is left unattended he can look hopelessly vulnerable. He must strike the right balance, try and assess the situation when and when not to move into midfield in order to support the play.

A winger stationary at a scrum or lineout usually has a large patch of the field to attend to. The full back, playing the middle of the park, cannot possibly cover the large open spaces on either side of him on his own. It is imperative that the wingers cover either side of him, but even if both wingers and full back are in good positions it still leaves a large area to cover. In such cases it is important for the winger to think of what might happen, to consider which part of the field he is in and the positioning of the opposite set of backs. Having played at outside-half and centre helped me as I had an approximate idea of what alternatives were open to my opponents in those positions. Positional sense is one of the most important requirements for a winger and allied to this is concentration. By getting into a good position in the first place he can save a lot of time and effort.

So on or near the halfway line, at the opposition's put-in at the lineout or scrum where they were likely to gain possession, I would not position myself as an orthodox extension of the open-side threequarter line. Instead I would go back five or six metres, almost behind the outside centre, giving a dog-leg shape to the threequarter line. In this position you rely a good deal on your own reading of the game resulting from past experience. You have lessened the chances of success of a kick over or through your own centres by the opposing outside-half or inside centre. You are also in a better position to counterattack. But if the ball is being passed along their line you must move up in line with your own centres, making a defensive line and getting closer to your own opposite number ready to move in to the tackle. This needs experience, confidence and an ability to read the game if you are not to be caught in no man's land by a kick ahead or to find yourself rushing up at the last moment to try and catch your opposite number.

If the lineout or scrummage is taking place closer to your own line, perhaps on the twenty-two, the open-side winger can take up a position which is more in line with the other two centres. Behind him is the in-goal area and if the opposition do decide to kick then it is a fairly easy matter for him to recover to touch down the ball.

If at the scrummage I was on the blind or narrow side

I always felt that it was wise initially to position myself very close to the scrummage. Before putting the ball into the scrum the opposition scrum-half could see that the so-called 'box' was unattended, so one of his alternatives was to kick into that position. However, once the ball had been put in and the opposition had hooked it, I would retire gradually to cover the box, with the opposition scrum-half now having to concentrate on the ball and on very little else. Positioning myself close to the scrum would also inhibit the opposition back row from attacking down the narrow side as they would already see me covering that possibility. In both cases it was a question of reading the game and trying to position myself so as to cut down the alternatives open to the opposition.

Alignment in attack tended to vary a good deal: sometimes I used to stand much deeper than the centres, at other times in line with them. This depended on the ploy to be used or on how much space I wanted to create between myself and my opposite number. For instance, it would be folly to align myself properly with the centres if I knew that the full back at some stage was going to come into the line. If the full back did come in it would leave enormous spaces at the back. So I had to position myself a little deeper so that if something did go wrong with the ploy and we did lose the ball, I was in a position to recover it.

I also aligned myself a little deeper in attack to create space. I have always felt that the man with the ball in space has the advantage because the defender has to wait until the man with the ball makes up his mind what he is going to do. Ideally, then, if I had the ball early on in a game I would try to go either inside or outside the man. On the second occasion I would try to do the opposite of what I had done the first time: perhaps a side-step on the inside first, then an attempt to swerve or run on the outside the second time. The idea was to create confusion in the mind of the defender so that on the third occasion he was not quite sure which way I was going to go. Once that happened the advantage was certainly on my side.

I always preferred to handle the ball very early on in the game. Even if I was tackled it was an opportunity to assess the ability of my opposite number: whether he was a good tackler, whether he was firm, whether he was quick and so on. There were occasions when I cherished a kick ahead and a chase after the ball. Then I could judge how fast my opponent was, what kind of runner he was, whether he was cumbersome, that kind of thing. Concentration in this respect was paramount. There was no use in idly chasing the ball; it was a chance to make some sort of assessment.

For myself I preferred always to play on the right wing. That was where I had started my career as a winger and that was where I always wanted to play thereafter. You get accustomed to the feel of the game, to playing on the one side of the field and you act or react accordingly. Furthermore my right foot was always the stronger. This was another skill which I could use in a close situation where I could not manoeuvre or side-step: I could as a last resort kick the ball ahead or make a cross-kick. While I would happily do this on the right wing, I would not have been able to do it on the left. More importantly, there was the comfortable feeling or 'field sense' of playing on the right and of having always played there. There were those who felt that I could only side-step off my right foot. In truth I could do it off my left as well, but if you are on the right wing you have more opportunity of side-stepping off your right foot and coming back into the field of play.

As a winger I had no real preference about the kind of centre that played inside me – the heavy, block-busting type or the small, elusive type. What was vital from

102

my point of view was that the centre had the timing and skill to give a good pass, and that he could do so under pressure. There is a misconception even amongst players that to give a quick pass is to give a fast, hard pass. This is not true. The kind of ball a winger requires is a quick ball but of a floating kind rather than a hard, low pass. The point is that the threequarters gain momentum as they run in attack and if the pass is a quick, hard one then it is very difficult to handle it. The French teams of the late 1950s and the 1960s were masters at passing the ball. The centres would perhaps be almost standing still. They would be lying so deep, the passes would float, and the momentum would come with the full back entering the line outside the outside centre. It seemed at times that the only people who ran were the full back and the winger. The line as a whole hardly moved. Emphasis was on superb passing and superb timing.

It is also essential for a winger himself to be able to pass inside and this more often than not requires the ability to do it one-handed. If you are tackled around the hips or the legs it is important to carry on the movement by passing the ball. If such a tackle was made on me then I invariably found that as I fell I would be able to pass almost off the ground with a one-handed pass from my right hand.

Finally, it cannot be said too often that coaches should not approach wing play in a negative way, concentrating excessively on what a winger should do in defence, the areas of the field that he has to cover and so on. If the winger is a gifted player then he should be looked upon in a positive way as a source of attack in the first instance.

7

The 1970–71 season was my second with London Welsh and whenever time allowed during the Christmas or Easter vacations, and whenever I had no commitments with the University, I played at Old Deer Park. Although I had known him for some time and had played with him on occasions, this was the time that I first came under the influence of John Dawes as coach and captain. You do not need to be a good captain or indeed a good player to be a good coach, nor do you have to be a coach to be a good captain. Yet in those halcyon days of the London Welsh era, the mid-sixties and early 'seventies, John Dawes did both jobs at Old Deer Park. In a sense he was very much in the old style of captain – as on the Lions tours of the past when the captain was responsible for being coach as well. John Dawes had a perceptive eye on the essentials of coaching, he knew how to conduct training sessions, he knew what he wanted of his team and at the same time, because he played, he had the sensitivity of a player. He knew ultimately his men's strengths and weaknesses and especially he knew the on-field pressures. Quite often a coach, sitting in the stands and looking objectively on the game, may not be fully aware of the problems on the field of play. Even a player who becomes a coach after his playing days are over can quite easily forget what it is actually like in the heat of the action. This is why it is so essential that the captain has a strong rapport with the coach. With John Dawes as coach and captain the discrepancy did not exist.

It is important that the captain should be recognised as the leader. It too often happens these days that the coach is assumed to be the one who controls the team, that he is looked upon as more of a figurehead than the captain himself. I have even heard it suggested that the coach should be allowed to go on the field at half-time to give his views and to suggest the tactics for the second half. This would be desperately wrong. Removing the mantle of responsibility from the captain's shoulders denies him authority. It is still a player's game and the captain should be chosen for his qualities of leadership.

John Dawes also had, and this was one of his strongest points, a broad vision of how the game should be played. It may be argued that in those days he had the players at London Welsh to play an expansive game; it is to his credit that he allowed this to happen. If it can be said that any one particular area formed the cornerstone of that gifted team, I would nominate the three back-row forwards, John Taylor, Mervyn Davies and Tony Gray. Whilst Mervyn controlled the back of the lineout and gave us plenty of possession, their most valuable work was in broken play. Both wing forwards were fast enough to get to any breakdown first, whether the movement broke down in our or in the opponents' threequarter line. These two inevitably arrived first to gain possession or to lend support and continue the attack and Mervyn, with his long, loping stride, would not be far behind. It was from this continuity that much of London Welsh's strength derived. Almost from then on I was convinced that in order to play open fifteen-a-side rugby it is essential to have a speedy wing forward, the type of specialist open-side wing forward which has almost gone out of fashion. This proved to be true at Cardiff later on where Stuart Lane, for all his niggly weaknesses, was such an asset. In this ccuntry at present we have become so concerned with our forward play, and with left and right wing forwards (their style being very similar) concentrating on the pincer defence on the opposing scrum-half, that we tend to sacrifice other aspects of play. A few seconds delay spent concentrating too much on the scrum-half can mean a lot of difference further out. Much of what is now being played resembles the brand of rugby which New Zealand made famous, and indeed the difference in styles that once distinguished countries is fast eroding. We may have learnt a lot from South Africa and New Zealand in the past, and in fact are contributing a great deal ourselves now, but have we lost something along the way?

John Taylor, whose value to the Welsh team has not becn fully recognised, and Tony Gray were also endowed with plenty of footballing skill, and that whole London Welsh side was full of exceptionally talented ball players. Of course John Dawes encouraged this to the full, devising moves from short penalties and counterattacks if the opposition tried a shot at goal. He discouraged a stereotyped response to any given situation: each position, whether in defence or attack, was one to respond to in a positive fashion, a challenge to inventiveness rather than a negative acceptance of what might seem inevitable. There were many occasions, sometimes several in one match, when we would run the ball from behind our own line after the opposition had attempted a penalty. At worst we would make fifty or sixty yards and at best, as did happen several times, someone would score at the other end of the field after the ball had gone through a dozen hands or so. Such moves demanded confidence as well as skill to execute and it was this inventiveness and adventure that particularly appealed to me.

It was no wonder that the crowds came in their droves from all over London to see us play. It was exciting, often unorthodox and relied a good deal on the calculated risk. I believe that the spectators and players enjoyed this kind of expertise. Whereas pattern play can bring its rewards it can too often become stale and repetitive. The joy of the game is to tempt the unexpected, to tease the imagination and test the skill not only of the opposition but of the players in your own team. To accept too readily a mechanical pattern of play can so easily mean accepting the lowest common denominator in order to achieve winning results.

I was to continue to play for London Welsh until 1974, but in 1971 there was a more pressing matter to consider: whether I would be able to make it to New Zealand for the Lions tour. My final exams in Cambridge were coming up in May and June and even if I were selected it did not look as if I would be able to make the first part of the tour for the couple of games in Australia. The four Home Unions had always stipulated in the past that the thirty players selected would have to take part in the tour from the very beginning. If this policy was to be pursued then I would not make the tour to Australasia. On the weekend that they were selecting the team I received a phone call from Carwyn James, asking me whether I could make it to New Zealand after the Tripos was over. If so, could I turn up for the week's preparations at Eastbourne, shortly before my examinations started? I willingly accepted those conditions, and so it was that I was selected to go to New Zealand in 1971.

Since rugby is an amateur game the greatest thrill it offers, apart from playing the game itself, is the chance to tour other countries. The game today knows no bounds. Whereas in the past, up until the 'sixties, touring was virtually synonymous with going on a Lions tour, nowadays all four home countries carry out visits, and clubs both great and small go on regular jaunts to overseas countries. What is also an experience is that for a time a player is, apart from the monetary aspect, a professional player; he can concentrate fully on the playing side of things without the external worries, distractions or responsibilities that he has at home. For six days in the week he can concentrate on either training or playing rugby football. On the Sunday he can rest.

No side that I have ever been with has trained on a Sunday; this was the day to travel to the next town and to relax. Training sessions of one form or another were held every day except when we were playing, so that, for instance, everybody trained on Mondays and Thursdays; Tuesdays and Fridays could be a light session, perhaps, for the Wednesday or Saturday team, but they were definitely days when those not involved in the playing side did train. Sunday, though, was a day when we could take a break from the rigorous routine of the other days, the bags were packed and the kit put away and forgotten for twenty-four hours. On the 1968 tour to South Africa it was also the day that John 'Tess' O'Shea called court to session and I acted as Prosecuting Counsel and Syd Millar acted as, well, we were never sure what duty he was to carry out. Anyway he was the senior member of the touring party so we allowed him to collect the fines which we imposed – usually a rand (50p) in the kitty, which went towards buying gifts for the management, for any friends we made in South Africa or for anyone having a birthday.

After the 1966 tour of New Zealand, when there were many accusations levelled, rightly or wrongly, at the Welsh contingent for being bad tourists and developing a Welsh clique, it was felt that holding a court would be one way of avoiding this kind of thing. Any minor indiscretions or lack of discipline could be penalised in full view of the players. For instance, anyone inappropriately dressed or not dressed in the regulation gear would appear in court. There was no need for the manager to reprimand anybody, no need for acrimony and bitterness. Instead the players carried out their own punishments. Of course, this was not meant to be taken too seriously and what might at first appear to be a serious transgression was found in front of the court to be humorous, embarrassing or both. It may sound puerile, but it did achieve its desired aim: no-one wanted to be brought up in front of court, in front of thirty-odd players to try and justify or defend any of the claims made against him.

Not least was the great hilarity it caused and with Tess as Chief Justice sometimes dressed in a sheet from his room, wound round him like a toga, it was often an uproarious occasion. Tess had the same instant kind of humour as Harry Secombe with the same high-pitched laughter, and towards the end of the tour the court became simply a vehicle for him to show his comic qualities. Maurice Richards, whose manners were exemplary, was brought to court finally for being too exemplary. This was too good to be true, the argument ran, therefore at some stage during the tour he must have committed some misdemeanour or other, even though no-one had caught him.

On the 1971 tour the Sunday school was the centre of attraction. Unlike the more staid and highly respected institution from which it took its name, the 1971 school was a group of people who gathered for a get-together over a few drinks on a Sunday evening. Initially it arose by chance that a core of the Lions had found themselves at a bar and from this regular meetings grew. We sang songs or played games of the kind that are traditionally fashionable in rugby club-houses like 'Buzz' or 'Names of . . .' Cliff Morgan eventually bought a dozen of us ties with the same design. On other tours perhaps this group could have been accused of cliqueyness but on this tour the camaraderie was such that nothing of the sort would have been thought of. On other tours much was made of the rule that you could not share a room with a fellow-countryman, and it was necessary to change rooms so that you did not stay too long with the same partner. In 1971 such distinctions did not matter much so in the end you shared with whomsoever you liked. The management had such a fine understanding of the players, and the players themselves had such maturity and confidence, that there was very little need for such trivialities as these.

As on all tours it was necessary to have a core of people who were by nature humorists, their spirit so unshakeable that they could be guaranteed to lift morale when necessary – not that the morale of this team was ever particularly low. Bob Hiller and Chico Hopkins, whose backgrounds were so dissimilar, struck up a relationship and repartee that always guaranteed almost constant laughter. The morning bus trip to training, not the most entertaining environment, became almost a music-hall act between the two. 'Boss' Hiller (known as 'Boss' because of his impeccable pedigree), your typical ''arlequin' as Chico pronounced it, supplied the dry ironic humour whilst Chico was the bouncy cheeky chappy. I am told that David Marques and Ray Prosser of the 1959 touring party enjoyed a similar relationship.

Chico was a particularly happy tourist. In some ways he had not expected to be chosen for the tour: Gareth Edwards was the automatic choice at scrum-half and he must have felt that it was unlikely that he would be chosen as another Welshman for the same position. When he was selected he vowed that he would grasp the opportunity to enjoy fully all aspects of touring. For the most part he achieved this aim but occasionally in his company I felt that something was niggling at the back of his mind, that he was not quite himself, that the humour was not quite there. It finally dawned on me what it was. On a British Lions tour, whether in South Africa or New Zealand, it is customary for each player to be adopted by a particular school. Pupils of the school normally collect a scrap-book of the tour which at the end of three months is presented to the player. In return the player makes special visits to the school when the Lions are in town to meet the staff and its pupils; it gives the children a lot of pleasure and is good for public relations. One item is more or less obligatory, which is that on the first visit to the town you attend the school's morning assembly to give an address. It was this that caused Chico some apprehension and uncertainty. He had not spoken publicly in his life and unfortunately he was not able to address his particular school until half-way through the tour, so on flights between towns he was to be seen scribbling away quietly on his own. The flamboyant extrovert turned into an almost reclusive introvert.

When the time came a few of us got up early with him to lend comfort at what was for Chico quite an ordeal. The speech went off extremely well and confirmed that the hours he had laboured over it were time well spent. He spoke quietly and at times effortlessly about Wales, about Maesteg and about the joy it brought him and the people of Maesteg for him to be chosen for a Lions tour. I shall never forget that he described Maesteg as 'a veritable paradise' – an epithet that I might not have chosen, perhaps, but clearly the town meant a good deal to him. Thereafter, the ordeal over, he resumed the ebullient comic role which he so thoroughly enjoyed.

As for Boss Hiller, such trivialities as making a public speech never concerned him. No occasion was too great, no circumstances beyond his mastery. Any man with pretensions to wit found his superior in Boss. Throughout the rugby-playing world there is that minority of followers who are arrogant, pig-headed and one-eyed, boasting about their own team's superiority and seeing no good whatsoever in the opposition. They are insensitive and sometimes callous in their remarks. These characters manage to exist everywhere, but there are quite a few in New Zealand and South Africa who have had the misfortune to come up against Boss. He could be subtle and witty or curt and sarcastic as the occasion demanded, but he was never offensive. Like was met with like. Whatever the occasion, it was Boss who had the final word.

From the very start of the tour Boss had accepted that with JPR in the party his role would be that of playing in the midweek matches. However, throughout the three-month trip he did hold one thing over JPR: whatever heroics JPR got up to on the field, however many tries he made or scored, Boss maintained good-humouredly that for all his strengths JPR was not a complete full-back. You do not achieve such status until you drop a goal, according to Boss, who had achieved quite a few in his time. There was the unforgettable moment, frozen in the closing shot at the end of the BBC film record of the series, after JPR had dropped that colossal goal from near the halfway line in the final Test at Auckland to draw the match and win the series. Running back, he turned to the stand with a broad grin and, lifting his arm, gave a thumbs-up sign. Some have thought that he may have been signalling to his parents who were there, others have interpreted it as a gesture to the manager to show that he had won the series. In fact he was giving a thumbs-up sign to Bob Hiller. With the final kick of the series, almost, he was turning to Boss for recognition of his feat.

All players enjoyed touring but none perhaps more than Gareth. He simply thrived on it. There were occasions when he became gloomy and introspective, usually as a

27. The victim of a short-arm tackle. The expression on Terry Cobner's and Ian Hall's faces show their exasperation. I wonder what's going through Ian Robertson's mind, on the right.

28. A good rugby friend: Jean-Pierre Rives, with (from right) Skrela, Paco, Cholley and Bastiat.

29–32. Wing play is not all about dramatic dives for the corner flag. You are often the last line of defence as well, and different situations demand different tackling techniques. A favourite tackle of mine came in the Wales v. France game

of 1972. Sillières, the French winger, not only had to be stopped, he had to be prevented from grounding the ball over the line and from making it available to his support.

33. Against Scotland in 1974. Going past **Andy Irvine and**
coming out of the side-step . . .

34. . . . fending off Nairn MacEwan, but to no avail. The
try line is still too far away . . .

35.　. . . but Terry ·Cobner is not. A pass from ground level
put him in for his first try for Wales in his first International.

36. Chasing a kick ahea
for the Barbarians v. Austral
in 1976. I always enjoye
playing for the Baa-Baas be
cause of the emphasis they p
on attacking, stylish rugb
I was finally honoured wit
the captaincy on the on
official occasion when th
British Lions played on Britis
soil – the Jubilee Match
Barbarians v. Lions, at Twic
kenham in 1977.

37. Playing against the Barbarians this time – for Cardiff,
in Cambridge blue, in the traditionally exciting Easter
Saturday fixture.

38. A proud and memorable moment, leading Cardiff onto the field to celebrate the club's Centenary. Garrick Fay (Australia) led the World XV and behind him is Tuisese (Fiji), followed by Valu (Tonga). The quartered colours were the original design for the Cardiff shirts at the beginning of their history.

39. A bearded Prince of Wales presents the cup and pennant for the Snelling Sevens competition in my first year as Cardiff's captain. Les Spence looks on.

40. Wedding day in 1971. The blushing bridesmaids are (from left) John Dawes, John Spencer, Mervyn Davies, Gareth Edwards and John Taylor. They are all wearing the 'Sunday school' ties presented by Cliff Morgan on the Lions' tour that year (see page 109).

41. With Cilla, Emily and Ben.

result of injury or of a performance which fell below his own remarkable standards. On such occasions there was a deal of self-questioning and doubt born of frustration, with anger seething just below the surface, but this was never directed at anybody else except himself. There was never apathy, which would have been a negative response; more than anything he is a person who looks positively on life and believes that it is to be lived to the fullest. He likes above all else to be master of the situation. If he felt on occasions that he had not quite mastered the situation on the field, then he would do so off the field. These black periods would never last for long, perhaps an hour or so after a match, then in our own team room when everyone else was excluded he would soon try some routine or other. His favourite was to take off his jacket and roll up his sleeves, turn up his shirt collar, brush his hair behind his ears, pull forward the front part just over his forehead to simulate the 'fifties style and go through his repertoire of rock 'n' roll songs. The Buddy Holly numbers would do for starters.

On such occasions Gareth superseded John Taylor who had been designated as choirmaster, a post in which he took so much pride. It was after one such evening that John was re-christened. At this time John not only had a fair length of crinkly hair but also sported a full-grown beard. Gareth during the evening was in full flow. Someone chipped in and asked, 'Hey, Gar, what about John? He's choirmaster, you know. You're not thinking of taking over, are you?'

'Oh,' said Gar, 'forget about him. Pick him up by his boot straps and use him as a brush instead – ay, a Basil Brush.'

John Taylor woke up the next morning to be known as Basil, or Bas for short. The name has stuck ever since. Bas remained choirmaster, however, as I do not think Gareth would have liked total responsibility. As long as Bas, who took the job seriously, allowed him his head now and again, he was happy.

There were many other occasions when I remember Gareth relishing the opportunity to give vent to his instant, spontaneous sense of mischievous humour. There was for instance the occasion on Wales' tour to Japan when on a morning bus ride to training he got up, picked up the driver's microphone and sang to the tune of Jimmy Dean's 1960s hit, 'Big Bad John'. Big Bad John (or Sid) in this case was John Dawes, our coach.

> 'Every morning at the field you could see him arrive,
> He stood five foot six and weighed 445,
> Kind of broad at the shoulders and broad at the hip,
> And everybody knew you paid no lip to Big Sid –
> Big Sid,
> Big Sid,
> Big fat Sid.'

And so on for a few more improvised verses.

The up-tempo songs or the raucous rock 'n' roll numbers were not always in favour, of course. It depended largely on the mood. Being so far away from home, a case could always be made for the slow, sentimental ballads with plenty of harmony, songs like the Everly Brothers' 'Dream' or Peter, Paul and Mary's 'Leaving on a Jet Plane'. There might be included some Irish rebel songs with Fergus Slattery to the fore, or some wistful Scottish ballad from Gordon Brown (or Stooky from Troon), or a Welsh hymn. If John Spencer, who was learning a Welsh phrase or two, had his way we would sing 'Sospan Fach'. Invariably the impromptu concert would end with Willie John standing up to sing 'Danny Boy' or some other quiet ballad with Irish connections, or perhaps Derek Quinnell doing fine justice to Frank Sinatra's 'My Way'.

That hour or two in our hotel after a match was always savoured and was almost sacrosanct. It was time away from the milling crowd, when we were out of the spotlight for once. We inevitably discussed the game up to a point but as far as possible John Dawes understandably and sympathetically tried to discourage us from doing so; plenty of time to talk later on in the night or the following morning or at any other time during the few days before the next match. Tomorrow after all was training time again and the machinery would be in motion preparing for the next match. And the next match, whoever it was, was always the hardest – we were constantly reminded, 'You wait till you get to Dunedin or Auckland or Canterbury or Pukekohe or Wellington' – or wherever – 'you wait, they're the hardest side.'

At the quiet end of the victory night Willie John would be there in his shirt sleeves. The large commanding figure, feared by many on the rugby field, would lend support to the general view, putting his arm around somebody's shoulder and saying, 'D'you know, I hate small men . . .' He would pause momentarily, look serious, but then with a broad smile and a glint in his eye, puffing at his pipe, '. . . but we'll forget that for now. Let's have a glass of potheen, a tale and tomorrow we travel on.' This great, gentle man, when I was caddying for him at the Wanderers golf course in Johannesburg in 1968, quoted as we walked down one of the fairways,

'I will arise and go now, and go to Innisfree,
And a small cabin build there, of clay and wattles
                                          made:
Nine bean rows will I have there, a hive for the
                                          honey-bee,
And live alone in the bee-loud glade'

and went on to finish W. B. Yeats' poem.

That to me was a marvellous memory and to some extent a testimony to the kind of man he is. I have memories of him, of course, as we all have, as an immense second-row player, an awesome sight in front of the lineout as he leans forward, slightly hunched, with a thick strapping of bandage around his forehead, waiting for the low, flat ball to be thrown in. But if I have another abiding memory of him, well, that too has nothing to do with the actual playing of the game. It is on the occasion of his last performance at the Arms Park for Ireland. The dinner and the celebrations are almost over and the whole evening is breaking up. Willie John is making his way up the stairs in the foyer of the Angel Hotel, with a few husbands and wives ready to drift towards home or collecting their keys to go to bed. Willie John stops, turns and starts singing 'Scarlet Ribbons'. He is asked for an encore and of course he sings the inevitable 'Danny Boy'. People stop, stand and listen. It would have been nice had other people been there to see that: the raucous, hearty side of rugby attracts the attention but there can be another side of the same coin which goes by almost unnoticed.

Touring is not all beer and skittles, or beer and song for that matter, there is the serious side of actually playing the game and playing it to win. The 1971 party struck the right balance of enjoyment and high seriousness in pursuit of a goal. Such a balance can only be attained through astute management, and Doug Smith never lost touch with the thirty players. By the very nature of his duties a manager is often away from the players and cannot spend all his time in their company. If he has an obsession about strict discipline he may interpret the smallest of misdemeanours as a major incident and may be too ready to clamp down and enforce regulations. This would not do on a tour containing thirty different personalities from varying backgrounds: it is not a military exercise after all, so a lot of leeway has to be given. It is to Doug Smith's credit that he maintained a steady course. In this respect he had exceptionally capable lieutenants in Carwyn James and John Dawes, who had their fingers on the pulse of the party. They were both sympathetic and sensitive to the players' needs and requirements and never at any stage did they pull rank except in a jokey way.

There was, it must be admitted, a certain reserve in Carwyn's make-up which kept him unwittingly at a certain distance from the players. He was always immaculately dressed for the occasion at whatever time of day it was, his hair Brylcreemed straight even in training sessions. The training sessions were also the only time he would not smoke his untipped cigarettes. He left a lot unsaid, but the moments of silence were as important as the moments of active talk and what he had not said was just as vital as what he had said. He never wasted words or ideas. At the very beginning of the tour he had said that he felt confident that we would win the series, and as the tour wore on and we got to know his style, we believed him.

Carwyn has no time for foolhardy ideas and out of this grows a supreme confidence. He is philosopher king in the coaching world, the complete antithesis of what many people imagine the archetypal coach to be. He is quiet and reserved. He talks reason rather than shouts commands. He prefers to coax rather than insist upon a response from a player. Whilst he values rugby as a great team game, he values above that the knowledge that the team is made up of individual players and that each one is to be treated with care and attention. Above all, each one is to be treated with respect. So many coaches treat the team as a group, but this is not Carwyn's way: each player, each set of new circumstances, would receive a careful and thoughtful response. So when Barry John, halfway through the 1971 tour, became tired of rugby training, Carwyn sent him away with Mike Gibson to kick a soccer ball about. Some people might consider this to have been preferential treatment of a star player but in fact it made sense: if the man was tired of it why not give him a break from the routine? What was important was his performance during a game. On another occasion John Pullin and Frank Laidlaw, our hookers, asked to go and visit a friend's farm for a couple of days and to be away from the team. Carwyn acceded to that request, too. I mention Carwyn in this context and not Doug Smith, our manager, because Carwyn, as coach, could have insisted that they turn up for training. Such requests were few, of course, but Carwyn treated each case individually and on its merit.

If it can be said that Carwyn failed in 1971, it was in the case of John Bevan, our winger. He had had an exceptional start to the tour, having scored ten or so tries in the first half-dozen matches. But being a raw youngster in 1971, he fell out of form, and form for John meant the act of scoring tries. He could have an otherwise brilliant game but if he did not cross the line, it made no difference what people said to him, John would be dissatisfied. After a few games such as this John became impulsive and impetuous, and the more these qualities manifested themselves the worse the game got for him. Carwyn tried all manner of things to get him to snap out of it but failed. A lot of players did, too, but I doubt very much whether anybody could have done anything in the circumstances. In the end John became dreadfully homesick and introverted and the last half of the tour was lost for him after that. Thus the President and Chief Operating Officer of Heinz, A. J. F. O'Reilly, when he has time to consider such momentous matters, can still sit smugly in his suite in Pittsburgh knowing that his record number of tries for a

Lions team in New Zealand may have been equalled but not broken.

Carwyn's confidence in his own ideas seemed to be extrovertly reflected in Barry John's play. Perhaps it's the water they drink in Cefneithin? And in the end I wondered whether Doug's prediction of two test wins to one and a draw was not Carwyn's idea in the first place, a lover as he is of theatre and drama. Was this prediction itself not some kind of poetic justice? Did we not leave these shores doomed to follow the path of so many other Lions tours? And when it looked as if the tour was going from strength to strength, did we not suffer the slings and arrows of the outrageous Canterbury pack the week before the first Test? When we seemed to be outgunned and outnumbered did not our defence remain classically and heroically intact in that vital Carisbrook Test? The bludgeon was kept at a distance by the rapier but only just; David had met Goliath and had won. When the tour was over there were those who said that the Lions had won because the All Blacks were not as strong as in the past, that they were in a period of decline. I doubt whether anybody would have said that after the first Test in Carisbrook when, although we eventually won, we had to survive typical New Zealand pressure in the second half. Winning that Test was vital, as Carwyn had pointed out beforehand. It first gave us confidence in our own ability and the gauntlet had been firmly thrown down; it was New Zealand who were being challenged. They were the ones who would have to come back from behind.

The tales started drifting back to us from Britain that there was a feverish interest throughout the land. We were winning and people were staying up at all hours listening to the reports. We could imagine, after losing the second Test, gentlemen in Surrey or Senghenydd who had heard it all before leaning back resignedly in their armchairs and saying, 'Well, we knew it wouldn't last long.' They returned soon enough to the edge of their seats when the third Test was over. It was there they would stay until a while after the very final blast of Referee Pring's whistle in Auckland, and they would say, 'They've done it, they've bloody well done it', half in jubilation, half in disbelief. But they were not to see JPR's upraised arms until much later – a pity, because that frozen image on the BBC film said it all for us and had a meaning beyond that of Bob Hiller's.

I have already mentioned the part that the manager, coach and captain played in the 1971 Lions' success. There was, too, the vital ingredient of experience. Mike Gibson and Willie John McBride had visited the country in 1966 and knew what to expect, and the hard lessons learned on the Welsh tour in 1969 were to prove invaluable. Statistically speaking, that 1969 trip could be considered a failure – it was a foolhardy tour to undertake in the first place with the first match against Taranaki taking place within thirty-six hours of arriving, and the first Test a week later. But the nature of the experience, rude awakening though it was for Wales who went there as European Champions, served us well in 1971. The Welshmen who went with Wales and returned two years later with the Lions were to form a not inconsiderable part of the team – J. P. R. Williams, Barry John, Gareth Edwards, John Dawes, Mervyn Davies, John Taylor and myself. With Mike and Willie, nearly two-thirds of the Test team had the vital experience. Ray McLoughlin had also been out to New Zealand in 1966 but unfortunately, after the Canterbury affair, he was not to take any further part on the playing side. All the same, he had exercised a good deal of influence on what was expected of the forwards.

The excellent spirit of the touring party provided the most advantageous atmosphere in which the players could show their talents on the field – and the 1971 Lions were not short of talented performers. If I have the space to single out only half-a-dozen of them in addition to those about whom I have written elsewhere in this book, it is in no way to detract from the others on that most successful of Lions tours to New Zealand.

There was of course the pack who carried out their monumental task. After the Canterbury game, when the likely Test prop forwards were physically wrecked, there were questions being asked as to whether we had a good enough second string to take their place. For the remainder of the tour both Ian McLauchlan and Sean Lynch created reputations for themselves and with John Pullin formed a marvellous foundation for the Test team. They with the rest of pack did much more than was originally expected of them.

Behind us all was the immovable J. P. R. Williams, whose commitment to a competition borders on the frightening. His immense presence gave us as a team strength and total confidence. New Zealand are fond of kicking the high ball at the full back to expose a team's vulnerability and destroy its morale. Most players, I am sure, are reluctant to deal with such a tactic and perhaps give only 75% of their commitment to it – the other 25% is thinking of what might happen. JPR gave 100% of his attention to the act of taking that ball. But more than that, once having retrieved it his thoughts were not entirely defensive and he would look to the options for attack. His style of play added another dimension to the role of the full back and to the possibilities open to any team in which he played.

Thousands of words have been written about Gareth Edwards and Barry John and whatever I say now would be superfluous. I simply admired and respected them. Apart from their immense ability, their instinctive knowledge of the game, their uncanny awareness of what was required at any precise moment in a match, their eye for an opening, the feel for the game's tempo and the confidence which they instilled into other players were of equal importance. These qualities which no coach could instil were simply in their blood. They knew what they could do and had the cheek and the audacity to do it. In temperament they were so very different. Gareth was dark, fiery and impulsive, his character feeding on the action around him both on and off the field. Barry was fairer, aloof and apart. Whilst the hustle and bustle went on around him he could divorce himself from it all; he kept his emotions in check and a careful rein on the surrounding action. The game would go according to his will and no-one else's, whereas for Gareth the adrenalin would flow according to the needs and the demands of the game. Each in his own way could dominate a match.

There was too the Gibson boy from Ireland, whose rugby was of an intellectual kind. Whereas Gareth and Barry's game had a supremely instinctive quality about it – the senses as opposed to the mind – C. M. H. Gibson applied his keen, almost academic mind to the proceedings. Imbued as he was with a wide-ranging skill, he could combine deft footwork and the occasional sleight of hand with a tremendous physical and mental commitment. His mind kept analysing and assessing so that he could remember the tiny details as well as the broad canvas of a game. Both mind and body were involved, and one felt that his total commitment would leave anyone else thoroughly exhausted and drained; such exactitude has no parallel. If this is any measure of the man, and it is, then he is well qualified indeed to pursue his chosen profession of the Law. But if this implies a dry, intense personality then it is only half the man, because in line with all Irishmen and most lawyers the other half has a terrific sense of humour. And the only vice he will admit himself is the occasional glass of champagne.

David Duckham of England had a rare footballing gift which served him well as a centre and as a wing. He was something out of the ordinary. More often than not you can categorise wingers (a dangerous thing to do, I suppose) into the small, speedy elusive type or the big, block-busting type. Duckham fell into neither category: he was tall, well built, he had strong hips and thighs but he was also very fast and, uncommonly for a big man, was able to use his feet deceptively. Witness his try for Coventry in the 1973 RFU Cup Final against Bristol and the number of times he ran and changed direction in the famous Baa-Baas v. New Zealand game in 1972, although on that occasion he did not score a try. He enjoyed side-stepping and swerving and was exceptionally good at both, so he was a difficult man to mark. What made it more difficult when competing against him, and perhaps I ought to whisper this quietly in case I lose friends in Wales, was that we became very firm friends. I found it difficult to muster the same competitive attitude towards him as I did towards others, and although this might be held against me by those who believe that such friendships should not determine a player's attitude in competition, the question never arose because whenever we played against each other neither of us had much of an opportunity to make the smallest contribution to the progress of the match. Be that as it may, he was the kind of man I would willingly meet, as did happen once, on the morning of a Wales v. England match to deliver some tickets which he desperately wanted.

Even after we had lost that torrid first Test we knew in ourselves that the 1971 Test series could be ours for the taking. It is one thing to think in this way but it is quite another thing to turn it into a reality: New Zealand teams, particularly the national team, have such a tremendous commitment to the game, such a strong will to win, that these qualities are difficult to overcome even with a highly skilful side. The 1971 Lions team had its own sense of commitment which was inextricably married to the qualities of skill and adventurous play. There were times when we wished for more regular, more steady possession, but we had said that if we could guarantee forty per cent possession, which was the vogue phrase at the time, then that would be enough. So it proved.

8

The 1971 Lions returned to Heathrow airport to a tumultuous and jubilant welcome from thousands of people who had travelled the length and breadth of England and Wales to welcome us home. Slightly dazed from the long trip and the celebrations on the aeroplane, we found at the airport scenes reminiscent of those occasions when the Beatles arrived anywhere.

There was another momentous occasion in that momentous year: within three weeks of arriving back in London I married Cilla White at Wimborne Minster in Dorset. Although I have not mentioned it so far in the book, I had met Cilla in the summer of 1968, soon after returning from that year's Lions tour and just before going up to Cambridge. It is curious how, after a long, hectic overseas rugby tour, it is very difficult to adjust to the ordinary, everyday routine. Life on a tour is so full of activity – training, travelling, playing, sight-seeing, official functions and so on, not to mention new experiences – that when one returns, both body and mind need time to re-adjust to a more staid and regular routine. One is in a state of limbo for a while.

It was whilst in this period of unwinding after the 1968 tour that I decided to go into Carmarthen for a change of scene. In the Ivy Bush I met up with Ken Davies, a BBC cameraman who had recently made a film of me after the return from South Africa. It was he who introduced me to Cilla, whom he had met when taking the photographs at a recent wedding where she had been a bridesmaid. Little did any of us realise then that the bridesmaid Ken had photographed that day would turn out to be the bride he would photograph three years later.

Curiously enough, photographs would play a vital part in our relationship. After that brief encounter we lost contact, as Cilla lived in Dorset and I was about to go up to Cambridge. Six months later, however, by pure chance, a Saturday match at Grange Road had been called off and I wandered into the Emmanuel College Reading Room. Glancing through the daily papers, I came across a face that was familiar. It was Cilla, who was freelancing as a model to raise some money prior to going to the Central School of Speech and Drama in London. I wrote her a chatty, 'do you remember me?' letter and with her move to London we were able to see each other more easily. Three years later, after my time in Cambridge and hers at drama school were over, we got married. Cilla's parents, Owen and Jo, had taken the entire responsibility for organising everything in my absence. After a four-day honeymoon in the Lake District we returned to settle for three delightful years at Christ's Hospital School in Horsham, Sussex.

Architecturally grand and sometimes imposing, set in vast acres of green land, Christ's Hospital was to be our home and teaching there my career for the next three years. The school was almost a self-contained community. As well as the ordinary academic teaching, which was done primarily in the morning, there was a great variety of sport to be played in the afternoons through the three terms. There were chamber concerts and exhibitions of various kinds. Many plays were put on throughout the year, some of them mounted on a very small scale by one of the houses, others arranged on a much larger scale altogether by the school. Regardless of the scale, the standard was very high indeed; the teachers as well as the children participated and it was indeed a corporate effort. There were highly talented teachers and very gifted children, and the beauty of it all was that it was not a public school in the accepted sense of the term. For a large majority of the children there were no fees to pay and what fees were paid by the others were very nominal, so the children came from a wide variety of different backgrounds. I did what I could to contribute to school life but invariably, as I had found in Cambridge, rugby took up a large part of my time. At weekends I played rugby but, unlike other schools, life continued in the Christ's Hospital community as if there was no weekend. Teaching was indeed a seven-day activity and I did what I could to make up during the week for any loss of time.

Although so much of my time was being spent on rugby, I did not consider it an intrusion as the years from 1971 to 1974 were among the most enjoyable of my rugby career; Wales were playing very much like a club team with a club spirit, and on Saturdays for London Welsh I enjoyed the excitement of playing their brand of rugby. What I also appreciated at London Welsh was that they played no midweek games so that during the week you could look forward very much to the Saturday match. I have always been a firm believer that you should only play once a week and that you should channel all your energies as a player towards that one big Saturday game. If a player has trained twice a week and already played a midweek game, there may be a sense of reluctance come Saturday to change into his kit for the fourth time in a week. By playing only once a week you keep a certain edge to your play which sometimes, if you play too often, can go a little blunt.

Because I lived and worked within Christ's Hospital it

meant, too, that I could train in my own time. There was
the occasional game of fives or squash and there was the
vast expanse of green that I could run in. Because I lived
forty miles away from Old Deer Park I could not always
make it to their training evenings but London Welsh were
very good in that they did not insist that I turn up for every
training session. I believed that I was conscientious
enough to make it up in my own way. This has been my
philosophy and I carried on with it when I came to be
captain of Cardiff. All I asked the players then was that
I should see them regularly at training sessions and I did
not insist that they turned up for every occasion. A player
was to be judged on his performance on the field of play
and as long as that was made clear to the player then I
was happy enough.

Above all, there was a wonderful spirit and sense of
camaraderie at Old Deer Park, not only amongst the rugby
players but in the club as a whole. Quite often, after our
first child, Emily, was born, we would go up as a family
because there was a crèche at the club to look after the
children while the game was on. Cilla, who had never
known anything about rugby football at the time I met her,
grew during these years to enjoy the game. She loved the
excitement, she enjoyed the company of its people, and
while it took me away from her for long periods, she has
been a constant source of encouragement. And when later
I took over the captaincy of Cardiff, she loved to get the
other players' wives involved in much the same way as they
had been at London Welsh.

There was always a sense of excitement in going to play
that one match a week, a sense of wanting to go out there
and play rugby. There was, too, the immense enjoyment
in playing for Wales. This was due partly to the success,
partly to the spirit and partly to being among familiar faces.
There was a passionate, almost obstinate, obsession in

wanting to represent Wales, a feeling which never deserted me to the end. I was to reflect later, after returning to Cardiff, that even though I felt passionately about playing for Wales there was a sense of relief in returning to the quiet and subdued atmosphere in Sussex. I was able to get away from it all and try to put the whole thing into some kind of perspective. While Gareth and Barry and the rest of the boys were left to their admirers I could wander anonymously down Horsham High Street without anyone knowing who I was. It would be untrue and grossly unfair to say that I did not like the admiration and the accolades, but it was satisfying at times to be able to remove myself to the cloisters of Christ's Hospital. Conversely, of course, there were times, particularly after a satisfying victory, when I wished that I could have stayed a little longer in the Welsh environment to savour it all.

The 1973 and 1974 Championship seasons were years of transition within this wonderful decade. During those two seasons nothing much was achieved. John Dawes and Barry John had decided to retire, Delme Thomas, Dai Morris, Jeff Young and John Taylor too had gone their separate ways. But 1975 brought its own quota of new players which gave impetus to the rise of another period of success. This was the year when the Pontypool front row began making their mark, Fenwick and Gravell provided a new pairing at centre and Geoff Wheel brought his own individual, idiosyncratic style to the team. It was the moment too that Mervyn Davies emphasised his ability as captain.

A captain may be chosen for a number of different reasons: he may be a forceful personality or a motivator, he may be a man who appreciates tactics and who can read a game, or he may command respect as a figurehead. Whatever his abilities, the important point is that the players under him should respond to him. Mervyn's main quality was that he set an example on the field of play. He did not say very much off the field and the few words he did say were straight and to the point so that no-one could mistake or misunderstand them. He simply led by example on the field and showed a total commitment to winning a game. He never asked anybody to do anything that he would not do himself. He was always in the forefront of all the action. Wherever the ball was, Mervyn was invariably there – gaining possession at the end of a lineout, or superbly controlling the ball at the base of the scrum, at the bottom of a ruck or making a last-ditch tackle. The only compliment I can pay him is that whenever he played I could never imagine anybody playing better as a number eight, either in years past or years to come. He seemed to have all the attributes required of that position. Number eights in the past have either been recognised as a third wing forward in that they were to be seen a lot in the open field or else they were primarily hard workers in the engine room. Mervyn combined both styles of play. And to think that when he first appeared in a Welsh trial it looked as if somebody had put a jersey on a clothes hanger.

In 1974 the time came for me to move once more back to Cardiff. I had decided that I should take a break from teaching, much though I enjoyed it, for the sake of my career. I had applied for a job and been accepted by the Sports Council for Wales to be one of their technical officers. Unfortunately, this coincided with the Lions tour to South Africa and I felt that it would be invidious of me to have resigned my post at Christ's Hospital and also to ask them for time off to go to South Africa. Mainly because my career was uppermost in my mind and there was a house to find in Cardiff, I felt that I could not possibly go to South Africa with the Lions. But the incident with my Cape Coloured friend in South Africa in 1968 had raised certain questions in my mind, although I have never been totally convinced that sporting isolation is a viable way of changing South Africa's abhorrent racial policies.

I therefore looked forward to rejoining the Cardiff club for the 1974–75 season after a six-year absence. Ever since I first joined Cardiff, playing for the club has always appealed to me. The crowd is less partisan than elsewhere: since Cardiff is more cosmopolitan than other Welsh towns, it is only part of the crowd that identifies fully with the whole team. In Llanelli, for instance, the majority of the crowd identify with Stradey because they are from that town or from the sorrounding area: in Aberavon the crowd is largely from Aberavon and so on throughout Wales. But Cardiff, being the principal city, draws its inhabitants not only from Cardiff and Wales but from all over the United Kingdom. There is a strong student community there, too, so that their partisanship and loyalty is unlike that of other rugby clubs. It seemed to me that the Cardiff crowd wanted something different from its rugby team – not merely a winning side but good, fluent, attacking rugby. Of course I may be wrong in this, but when I took over the captaincy in the 1975–76 season I started off with this premise – which in fact suited me down to the ground because that was what I wanted, too. This is not to say that I did not want to play winning rugby. Of course I did, but I did want it achieved in a certain style. My philosophy was and still is that if the opposition score two tries then we will score three tries – barring penalties, of course!

I would like to think that in the three years that I was captain I satisfied both sets of customers: the indigenous Cardiff contingent and those from out of town. When I arrived back in Cardiff there was one common complaint: Cardiff had lost their glamour, they were not playing in the style to which they had grown accustomed in their hundred-year history. Something had gone wrong and had been lost on the way. It may have been presumptuous of

131

me but I did intend to go part of the way to putting it right. I like to think that we achieved a certain adventure in our style of play. In recent years it has become fashionable to refer to the Welsh team as a machine – this was a compliment in that there was something inevitable and predictable about the outcome and indeed it was remarkable to think that an International XV could perform in such a way as to merit this description – but I must admit that if this was applied to a club team that I captained, I would not be entirely happy. A side needs cohesion and understanding, with each cog fulfilling its function, but I would also expect a flash of individual skill – I would expect the unexpected, if you see what I mean. To be labelled a machine would have too much of the production line syndrome about it: there would be a quality of sameness which would ultimately produce boredom and monotony. The players need something more than this, and the spectators in order to be entertained want something different, not a repetition of a previous performance. The crowds want star performances, they enjoy the idiosyncrasies of players; the very definition of a machine would preclude all this.

I was aware that it is not always possible to play an expansive sort of game, that the weather may be against you, the conditions heavy. In that case you adapt your style of play accordingly, but it is none the less important to set objectives. In that first year of captaincy progress was slow and unsure, which was only to be expected; after all, I was a new captain, I had to have time to get to know the players and the players in turn had to get to know me. It took time to gain their confidence and time also to impart to them my ideas of how I wanted the game to be played. I was fortunate enough to have in both John Evans and Chris Padfield two coaches who had similar ideas and I am immensely indebted to them. And, of course, there were the players themselves, many of whom were quite young, who made a terrific contribution to the style of play. They were a great bunch who enjoyed themselves on and off the field and made my job as captain much easier.

I was also fortunate in the support I received from the Cardiff committee. In particular, Les Spence became a close confidant over the years and has proved an admirable administrator. Although an elder statesman in the game in Wales, he is still very much in touch with present-day thinking about the game and its likely future development. Unlike a lot of other administrators he does not harp back too often on the old days; it is the present that concerns him and what happened in former years is only one yardstick by which any further developments can be judged. He and his wife Babs are wonderful people. Babs is endowed with a terrific sense of humour, sometimes witty and subtle, and on other occasions very risqué. I must admit that she is the author of one of the anecdotes I use frequently in my after-dinner speeches. When Les was President of the WRU, Babs was accorded the reception and hospitality which went with her husband's status. When someone at RFU Headquarters (HQ is always the butt of these anecdotes in Wales, I'm afraid) turned to Babs and said that he thought that England might do very well this year because 'you see, we have a new coach', Babs turned to him and retorted, 'That's all very well but it's not how you get to the ground that's important, it's how you play on it!'

I was confronted several times in the Cardiff clubhouse by people who commented that I ought to be more robust in my approach, that I ought to stamp my authority on the team. There were supporters who were desperately wanting success and wanting it quickly, so they felt that the more authoritarian attitude was the answer. What they failed to understand was that their way of doing things was not my way and it needed a different personality to do it how they wanted it done. I preferred a quieter and what I thought a more reasonable approach; 'This above all, to thine own self be true'. On occasions I did exert my authority but there was a time and a place for it and I certainly was not going to be influenced to veer off the path that I had set myself. I had a good enough idea of what I wanted to be done and I knew roughly how to set about it.

Having listened to quite a number of club coaches and captains give their final briefings I have come to the conclusion that they are much of a muchness, although there was never any sense of déjà entendu at international level. It seems that games are always important, that it is always vital to win them. There is a great profusion of once highly regarded Anglo-Saxon words which now have lost their effective currency. They are casually used as nouns and adjectives and are meant to whip up the necessary motivation. To swear continuously is the vogue and is meant to make for a highly charged pre-match talk. But in my opinion it was always important in team talks to adopt a different approach for each match, to emphasise different aspects of play and to give a realistic appraisal of the particular match in hand. It is always important to be as sincere and as realistic as possible, for otherwise the players in your charge would soon see through you. It is important, too, to be aware of certain problems, like for instance playing under floodlights. A player may be off form or perhaps after a particularly hard day's work he is not prepared mentally or physically for a game. These things should be taken into account. It is not as if they are professional players, after all.

It is not only what you have to say beforehand that is important but also what you have to say after the match. It is essential to maintain a positive note in after-match comments, to praise the side's efforts rather than emphasise weaknesses. Being negative can provoke tensions and possibly increase any tendency to aggression. In the same way, it is essential to be positive about the opposition.

My one regret from this last period of my rugby career is that I would have liked to win the Welsh Rugby Cup for Cardiff, for in most people's eyes that is a measure of a successful team. But I wonder sometimes whether winning the Cup would have given me more satisfaction than to hear and read people say that Cardiff were the most exciting team in the land. This was good news indeed and had a sweet sound to it, but had I accomplished that which Cardiff have yet to accomplish, it would have been a complete vindication of what Chris Padfield, John Evans and I were trying to do at Cardiff.

The Cup competition in Wales is after all a tremendous competition. It allows the smaller clubs to compete against the big ones. It allowed Cardiff, for instance, to go up to a village like Garndiffaith and come away victors by no more than three penalties to nil. Such matches also indicate the value of coaching: whilst the progress made by the major clubs through coaching has been increasingly apparent for all to see on television, it is during the Cup competition that we can see that the smaller clubs have also benefited and been enriched by the coaching system. The tension of a big match and the occasion of a home fixture against a side like Cardiff can raise the spirits and the competitiveness of a small side like Garndiffaith, but in that particular game it was made clear that the principles and techniques of scrummaging and mauling, for instance, had been thoroughly digested and were being put into practice. Their approach was not merely that of a highly spirited and motivated team.

Before the game, I must admit to my embarrassment, I had not even heard of Garndiffaith. When Les Spence, the Cardiff committee man, rang me to announce who our opponents were to be in the next round of the Cup, I had to ask him, thinking perhaps that his pronunciation of Welsh names was not what it should be, to spell out the name slowly letter by letter. I admitted to being none the wiser. This is in no way meant to be derogatory or irreverent, merely ignorance, pure ignorance! Clearly my knowledge of geography was not what it should be. At any rate, that Saturday's closely competed match ensured that I would not repeat my mistake and proved conclusively that the lessons of the coaching manual had penetrated even this outpost at the head of one of the Gwent valleys.

The Cup not only allows for the big clubs to play the smaller clubs but it is good in that it unifies rugby throughout the land by bringing the south and the north of Wales together. It also adds a finer edge to the competitiveness that already exists in Wales in the regular matches that take place between clubs in the area, without (so far at any rate) adding so much keenness that the games deteriorate and spill over into violent behaviour. Some of the most exciting club games that I have ever taken part in have been in this competition.

The Cup adds just the right amount of spice to a mixture which already has a great deal of flavour, but to impose a league system upon that which already exists would be folly. Whereas the Cup competition arouses the right kind of needle four or five times, if you are lucky, in any one year, the continuous pressure of play for points could have an inhibiting effect on the style of play and on everyone's enjoyment of the game. It can be argued, of course, that by imposing the one you need not neglect the other but I disagree; in theory it might be so but I doubt very much whether it would work effectively in practice. If such a league did come into existence the very nature of rugby in Wales could have to change, particularly as there would be such an emphasis placed on promotion and relegation and on playing for two points. Its only advantage would be to give the smaller clubs an opportunity to become bigger clubs, but I doubt very much whether it would increase the number of big clubs.

I question, too, whether the players would actually enjoy it; playing for points would inevitably increase the pressures. I have yet to be convinced that leagues, either in France or Scotland, have added to the enjoyment of the game, and since it still is an amateur game enjoyment is a prerequisite. The close proximity of the clubs in South Wales means that each game there has a local derby flavour about it, so that the keen edge of competition is ever present. To superimpose a league system on what is a very natural structure could endanger the healthy rivalry that already exists and to add points would seem an artificial imposition on something that has grown naturally out of the Welsh environment. Clubs could suffer ignominy by their relegation, a deeply felt embarrassment and bitterness in not gaining any winning points, and no club in an amateur set-up should suffer such things.

I have been surprised in the past to hear coaches, even of the smaller clubs, saying that in some respects these days they are considered within the club in much the same way as soccer managers, that it is they and not the players who have to take much of the burden of criticism after a defeat. Some of them therefore believe that if they are going to get such pressure then it may as well be in a league system. Yet a coach can only be as good as the captain and the players he deals with. He is not the answer to all ills on the rugby field, he is only part of a larger entity. In any case, a league would only exacerbate the situation and not alleviate it. The players would also come under a similar pressure to improve their performance, which would certainly not be fair on men who have other more important things to occupy their minds in their daily lives.

Others argue that one officially recognised league would do away with the proliferation of other leagues and pennants which are now in existence. The essential difference is that if a league were officially recognised the clubs would have little choice in the matter, whereas now a club has the alternative of opting out, except from the Western Mail Championship, which is based on every game during the season played by one of the top sixteen Welsh clubs, whenever it takes place and whoever the opposition. I believe that this has its value. In the end it can be dismissed as unofficial, and quite frankly it does not truly indicate the overall superiority of the winning side, but it creates an interest for most of the season. At the end of the season it only pleases the one solitary team, the winner, and even then it is a dubious distinction. It does not please all the people all the time, nor does it please some of the people all the time, nor even all the people some of the time; it merely pleases some of the people some of the time. Clubs recognise it when it pleases them; those who do well pride themselves on the fact, those who do not do so well take comfort from the enormous discrepancy in the quality of the opposition on certain clubs' fixture lists. Its very unofficialness, curiously enough, is its abiding quality. For the losers the escape clause will always be that it is not officially recognised and that they therefore need not lose any sleep over it.

Of the two ambitions I set myself as captain of Cardiff – to win the Cup and to develop a style of play which would please the fifteen players and thrill the Cardiff crowd – I like to think that we went a long way to achieving the one, but disappointingly we fell on or very near the final hurdle in the other. Winning the Cup remained a particularly enchanting dream, its full realisation and accomplishment as elusive as a charming guest.

9

Take a dream and let the dream come true. Take a fanciful boy who dreamed of playing for Wales and of playing the sport in which folk heroes are born, a sport to which a country is devoted and of which its people are particularly proud. Take a dream which countless others dream but for whom it can only remain obscure and intangible. A child's dream can become the adolescent's idealistic aim, and the young man can make it into an achievement. Let the young, green years roll away and the dream becomes a reality.

Take the game which Wales played against Scotland in Murrayfield in 1971, and the manner it was played – the lead changing hands several times and the whole epic being settled by John Taylor's famous conversion. Was not that the essence of a dream? And take the Lions tour in the same year to New Zealand. Success was finally achieved where so many others had failed, and Doug Smith's prediction became fact – was not that too like a dream come true? At times, it has gone beyond anyone's wildest dreams. The Grand Slam has been achieved on three separate occasions and the Triple Crown won in three successive years. To take part in games when Barry John reigned supreme; to be present when Gareth Edwards scored his try against Scotland at the Arms Park and returned mud-bespattered while Spike Milligan went into a frenzy; to be part of the movement which led to Phil Bennett's try at Murrayfield in 1977; to play in epic encounters against France for the European Championship – were not all these the stuff of dreams? It has all come true and Wales has enjoyed a decade of unparalleled success.

Yet it seems strange that the dreams were fostered and they flourished on the field called Parc-y-Ty in Llansaint. The first sign of encouragement came unwittingly from the boys in the village – my name being the first called out when picking up sides was an indication that I had some skill. There were other signposts along the way – a teacher giving encouragement, a mention, however slight, in the local newspaper, the adults taking an interest in matches which I played. Being asked, too, by either Carmarthen Athletic or Kidwelly to play for their teams, getting a Secondary Schools cap, or being invited to play for the Welsh Academicals. All these were encouraging, tell-tale signs along the way. But skill must be harnessed to motivation and motivation must come, not from the teacher, or coach, or friend (although these are necessary), but from the deeply-felt ambition to achieve.

December 1967 was a culmination of a kind, that first cap for Wales against Australia. It was the ultimate accolade, the final recognition. But as well as an end of something it was a beginning, too, a new starting point. It was also a challenge to go on proving, for a while at any rate, that I could do it more than once. Then it was a desire to go into double figures and for a time, unfortunately, it became almost a statistical exercise. Playing for Wales then did not provide an all-embracing satisfaction. The new impetus came under Ray Williams, whose contribution to Welsh rugby is immeasurable, and under the guidance of Clive Rowlands as coach. Gradually, as a result of the influence of these men and the wisdom of the Big Five's selection policy, Wales started playing as a confident unit with a pervading team spirit and atmosphere. There were occasions before this when four or five changes in a Welsh team would not cause raised eyebrows, but in the late 1960s there were very few changes, if any, made to the team. A confidence grew out of knowing that the team selected itself, that the same fifteen or thereabouts would take the field time and time again. Players knew each other, the selectors were just as familiar, and it became an identifiable squad instead of merely a motley collection of club players who went out to represent Wales. Players were recognised for being the Welsh team. Dai Morris may have played for Neath, Mervyn Davies and John Taylor were London Welsh men and Jeff Young played for Harrogate, but more than that the first three were the Welsh back-row forwards and Jeff Young was the broad-chested Welsh hooker. And so it was for all the others. They had all played so often that the Welsh team was itself a club.

Although the first of the five Triple Crowns was won in 1968–69 and the Championship shared in 1969–70, it was in 1971 with the first of three Grand Slams that the team came of age and the value of the squad training policy was seen. In achieving the Grand Slam in that year Wales had to beat France in Paris. Whilst it is always more difficult to win matches away from home it is beating France in Paris in the spring that is a supreme test of skill. This was what we did in 1971, in what Ray Williams still maintains was the greatest Championship game that he has ever seen.

Wales have managed to win twice altogether in Paris in the 1970s and it is only Ireland (once) of the other countries that has managed to secure a victory there. In order to maintain a good record in the International Championship it is imperative to win the home matches (Wales have not lost a Championship match at Cardiff in the 1970s), but to win such things as the Triple Crown and the Championship it is of course vital to win away matches. In this, too, Wales have been successful: they have won eleven out of seventeen away games, England three, Scotland two, Ireland five and France seven.

It is here that the true measure of the Welsh team lies. There is much talk of the influence that the crowd has on the effectiveness of the Welsh team; it is said that the team feeds off this support and that the crowd at the Arms Park is a source of inspiration. This is quite true, of course, but if a team is to be successful it will be largely because of its inherent skill and its strong character, and these qualities are best shown when playing in away fixtures.

France always perform confidently and expertly on their own patch, as do Scotland, who always find an extra yard of pace at Murrayfield. Like France, they seem reluctant, more introverted players when playing away from home. In the 1970s Scotland and Wales have played three terrific games of rugby football – 1971, 1975 and 1977 – the outcomes of which were not settled until the dying moments. Not only had they cliff-hanging climaxes but they were also games full of skill and expertise, plenty of adventure and good rugby. The drama at the end – John Taylor's conversion in 1971, Alan Martin's failing with the conversion in 1975, and Phil Bennett's try in 1977 – added to the overall excitement. The games stick out in my mind not only for those moments of drama but for the fact that Scotland were prepared to keep on the attack, unlike a lot of other games when the opposition's prime intent was to stop Wales. Curiously, Scotland seem unable to reproduce the same form or style when they come down to Cardiff.

Ireland were another team imbued with a terrific Celtic fervour when playing at Lansdowne Road. They were not always fortunate enough to have their full quota of skilful players – in fact the Irish themselves were fond of saying that they could find eleven players of International calibre but they would be struggling to fill the remaining four places. Whatever the team, they would play as if their bellies were on fire, their hearts more often than not ruling their heads. Such emotion, no doubt inspired and motivated in the dressing room, would be maintained relentlessly for eighty minutes. Whereas at the Arms Park we felt as a team that we would have to survive their onslaught for twenty minutes or so, after which the fire would subside, it would be foolish of us to think that the same applied at Lansdowne Road. At Cardiff there would usually be a breaking point but there was no chance of anything of the sort happening in Dublin.

At no time was this truer than in the Triple Crown match in 1978. It was not a game played in the best of spirits, in fact it was frequently an ill-tempered affair. When the Irish came back to draw level at thirteen-all their tails were up and dreams of that triple Triple Crown for Wales were fading fast. It is at those precise moments that a team needs to play with more than just the heart, with more than just passion. You can come out of the dressing room feeling such inspiration but halfway through the second half it is very difficult indeed to summon up the right emotions. At those moments you need to play with skill and with a cool head. It needs courage, of course, but it must be allied with tactical nous.

Curiously enough there was no jubilation in the Welsh dressing room after that victory, no immediate sense of celebration. The players were drained after the final few minutes' effort on the field. I wonder what the Big Five thought of the scene that confronted them when they walked in to congratulate the team on its success. The players still had their jerseys on, a good quarter of an hour after the final whistle, and there was complete silence. It was Cliff Jones who finally tried to break that silence. He said, 'You may not realise it now, it may take time for you to appreciate it, but in ten, in twenty years' time, you will be the team that won the triple Triple Crown. You've made history.' By the time we finally reached the Shelbourne Hotel the idea was beginning to seep into our consciousness. But it did take time.

If I said earlier that Irish hearts ruled Irish heads I must add that the most intense and most detailed thinkers that I have ever known in a game have come from Ireland – men like Ronnie Dawson, Ray McLoughlin, Mike Gibson, Syd Millar and Tom Kiernan. These marvellous people had a passionate love of the game which could involve you in hours of detailed discussion.

If the Irish selectors had the problem of not having enough players to fill their international team, England seem to have had a problem of a different kind, one which they have not been able to resolve during the last ten years. They cannot make up their minds from the great fund of players available who exactly their best players are, and what exactly is the best permutation.

There were awry English selections during the 1970s. There was an indecisive and unpredictable selection policy which translated itself into unsatisfactory and unsure play by the English team. This was only to be expected as a lack of confidence in selection inevitably leads to a lack of confidence on the field of play. You were never quite sure who was going to be in the team next time. There were players who one would have thought should have appeared regularly in the English jersey but who only appeared intermittently. Other players were given the initial opportunity but never allowed to gain in confidence. Still others were dropped when they were beginning to gain maturity after having been given the necessary initial experience. It was all so haphazard and unpredictable and the team's performance reflected this. Players were not allowed to mature together in a cohesive unit. There was a hesitancy and unsureness among the English players because they were never sure whether the game they just played was to be their last or not. And if it was their last chance, then they would go into oblivion for a while.

The prime rule of selection, particularly of an international team, is that a player is not replaced until you are sure that there is a better man on the sideline. You do not pick a new player in the hope that he might be better than the man dropped or to change for the sake of changing. You have got to be sure that he is better.

It saddens me to think of what happened to the Duckham and Spencer pairing in the centre. For two or three years they were the golden boys of English rugby but after 1971 they were split up. David Duckham had a highly successful tour in New Zealand on the wing, John Spencer had a less happy time on the field; the Lions team after all had an exceptionally wide choice in the backs. There was no reason why they should not have continued as centres for England, but once the tour was over David Duckham played on the wing for England, where he was starved of opportunity, and John Spencer went into oblivion. 'Spence' went back to his beloved Wharfedale and in recent years it is only through the grace of the Barbarians that he has been able to keep the same company again, company in which he rightly belongs. Not only that, but I always felt that in John Spencer England had a man who would have served them well as captain during a time when they needed a figurehead. He was not endowed with Duckham's flair but they did complement each other very well. Unfortunately the selectors did not consider the strengths of the pairing; they preferred, rightly or wrongly, to emphasise their defensive weaknesses.

The more I think about it, the more I realise not so much how the backs are dependent on the good pack of forwards and vice versa, but how individual players are dependent on one another. Players feed off each other, the one player complementing the other. A player is good because of somebody else inside him, he reacts instinctively to somebody else in particular. Think of Edwards and John, Edwards and Bennett, Dawes and Gibson, Butterfield and Davies, Hastie and Chisholm, Marques and Currie and, sadly because it was not allowed to come to fruition, Duckham and Spencer. Considering the amount of possession England have managed to gain from their forwards in recent years, Duckham and Spencer would have flourished in the English jersey. A great opportunity went astray and possibly some great moments of English rugby were missed.

People frequently ask me which one of all the wingers I faced was the most difficult to mark. I always thought that Bryan Williams of New Zealand was a dangerous and effective winger to play against. He was stockily built and very fast, with a devastating side-step off his left foot, but for some reason known only to themselves the New Zealanders quite often picked him on the right wing. He was a more effective left winger than right winger because of the side-step coming back into the field of play. There was Keith Fielding of England, but he was not picked often enough for me to make a full assessment of his play. But most certainly the winger I respected and admired most was David Duckham, about whom I have already written in this chapter and in the chapter on the 1971 Lions tour.

For me the players who have given the greatest pleasure are those who have been able to run and to pass accurately to create space, who use their hands, eyes and minds to create time and their bodies to deceive and manoeuvre. I have never been enamoured of the player whose only subtlety is to run at the opposition in the hope that muscle and body weight will create space and opportunity by using the so-called crash ball. Such a move has its rightful place in the game, I admit, but it was the other kind of player that I admired the most, the kind which is epitomised by the delicate virtuosity of Phil Bennett, whose three audacious side-steps for the Barbarians against New Zealand in 1972 will live for ever in the memory; or by the easy gliding motion of J. J. Williams in full flight; or by the deft artistry of Scotland's Andy Irvine and Ian McGeechan.

There are the forwards, too, who make it possible for the runners to display their skills: the likes of Charlie Faulkner, Bobby Windsor and Graham Price; 'Mighty Mouse' McLauchlan, Sean Lynch and John Pullin, who plough their own particular furrow. It is above all a team game and the ball-winner and the ball-user are dependent on one another: the one produces efforts of heroic proportions and the other the drama. But there are also forwards who like to run with the ball and show a touch of back-division skill – men like Derek Quinnell, whom I have yet to see commit a misdeed on the field. He is a forward who has played at the highest level in three different positions in the pack, each one considered such a specialist position. Remember the way he picked up the ball off his ankles for that great Barbarians try against the All Blacks in 1973, and his similar display of skill for JJ's try against New Zealand in the Christchurch Test in 1977. There was also the running of Graham Price for his try in his debut match against France.

Then there are those who ask me about my favourite try. This is always a difficult one to answer. One try can be appreciated for some touch of skill, another can give pleasure because it was a vital try, scored at a crucial stage in the game, a third because it finishes off a particularly satisfying movement. Certainly, it gave me as much pleasure to create a try, to execute a particular skill which made the opportunity for a try to be scored, as to score one myself. I can remember the pass I gave to Terry Cobner for his first try for Wales on the occasion of his first cap against Scotland; and the pass I gave to Clive Burgess of Ebbw Vale, also on the occasion of his first cap, against Ireland; and running the ball out of defence at Murrayfield in 1977, to begin a movement which ultimately led to Phil Bennett scoring against Scotland. These were touches which gave genuine satisfaction, more than some of the tries I had scored. The wing is so often looked upon as just the scorer of tries, taking the ball over the line after somebody else inside him has done most of the creative work. Perhaps it was a carry-over from my days as a centre that I so much enjoyed the creative side of the game.

Quite naturally, scoring a try gives its moment of elation because ultimately it serves the team by adding to the scoreboard, translating into points a team's effort. Demonstrating a particular individual skill gives a more egotistical sort of satisfaction because there is pride in performing it. Sometimes there is an element of luck which takes something away from a particular try – a mistake made by the opposition or the bounce of the ball, for instance – but when you run with the ball in your hands you invariably create your own chance by a change of pace or a side-step. You quickly analyse the opposition, the number of players covering and their speed and angle, so that the mind can analyse the options that are open. Quickness and accuracy of thought are of prime importance in selecting the right option. There are other occasions, and this is less easy to analyse, when there is no time at all and you rely on an instinctive reaction.

If I were able to state categorically which was the most unforgettable try, it would not say very much for twelve years' experience in International rugby or fifteen years' experience in first-class rugby. Maybe the first two tries that I ever scored for Wales should have been indelibly printed on my memory, but they have gone astray and I cannot recollect them. Perhaps it is because they were overshadowed by other events that day which were thereafter encapsulated in the name, Keith Jarrett. I could not possibly have rated them very highly. There was a try against England in 1971 which I would not have considered important but for the fact that it was my first try on the wing at Arms Park. It was quite simply a twenty-five yard sprint for the corner flag. Yet there was a try against New Zealand in the Third Test in the same year, from a much shorter distance of seven or eight yards, which I shall never forget because, first, it was a vital score and, secondly, it was in an enclosed space with a couple of defenders in the way of the line. There were tries against Hawkes Bay in the same year, and in my final year for Cardiff, 1977–78, there were tries against Pontypool and against London Scottish and the try in the Sam Doble match at Moseley which for several reasons gave particular satisfaction.

Well though everything was going at club level during that 1977–78 season, I began to have thoughts about calling it a day. The International matches for me personally were undistinguished. I wondered then whether to take part in another season. If I did, would that season be one too many, and would a sense of repetition set in? Then I asked myself, could I not forgo International matches and limit myself instead to club rugby? Was not the Welsh cup still to be won by Cardiff? But when the time came to make a decision it was a case of all or nothing. Dropping out of International matches, so I reasoned, might mean a drop in standards, and if I played only at club level could I face another long winter of training and playing without the

" SPREAD IT AROUND, HE'S SAYING A COUPLE FOR GERALD ! "

(This cartoon appeared during the week leading up to the Grand Slam match against France in 1978. In the end, no amount of prayer could help me, and a hamstring injury did force me to withdraw from the team.)

added impetus of a Welsh jersey in January? No – the blood had danced for too long to that particular tune.

Colin Howe, a committee man at Cardiff, once said that you prove yourself a rugby player on a wet, windy, Wednesday night at Maesteg. Dave Rollitt, the former England forward (I say 'former' but he is still playing and may yet be called to arms) was also once quoted as saying something similar: 'An Englishman can count himself a good rugby player if he can go down to Aberavon on a wet, winter's evening in January and play well', or words to that effect. Neither of these remarks tells the whole story, but all generalisations have a grain of truth in them and I can see what both Howe and Rollitt mean. However difficult or insurmountable the odds may seem, you must still retain an unquenchable spirit for the game, a keen competitive attitude and a belief that players' skills can overcome those odds. It is all very well to jink and dance about in the clear autumn in the open spaces of Richmond Park to the polite applause of a genteel crowd but it is quite another matter to do the same thing elsewhere in treacherous conditions or at an awkward time of day.

In September 1978, when I decided to call a halt to the training and the playing of rugby football, the weather was fine, the grass was recently mown and fresh, and I saw Cardiff play against the local district side in a free-running, high-scoring game. But there was no desire to join in, no urge to play, so what would it be like in dark November to pull my boots on for a midweek away match in the conditions described by Colin Howe and Dave Rollitt?

The time had indeed come to put my boots away in a warm comfortable place, but if our newly born son, Ben, ever felt that he wished to play the game then I would not discourage him. Without rugby I would not have known moments of triumph such as the Fourth Test in 1971 when the series was won – nor moments of disaster when Wales lost on the tour of New Zealand in 1969 and Australia in 1978. I remember the moment of happiness when first picked for Wales, the moment of sadness when I was dropped in 1968 and no reason given. I remember the moment of elation when I first captained Cardiff, the moment of despair when I dislocated my elbow for the second time in 1969 against France at Stades Colombes and was advised to give up the game. I remember moments of sheer excitement, as when I flew into Cape Town for the first time and saw Table Mountain, or landing in that extraordinary place called Hong Kong. I remember with pleasure the time spent in the company of the Fijian team at the Royal Cambridge Hotel singing 'Isa Lei', listening to their harmony and marvelling at their exuberance and vitality. I remember the distinction of captaining the great Cardiff Rugby Club in their Centenary year and speaking before a thousand people in a candle-lit marquee in the grounds of Cardiff Castle. I remember visiting 10 Downing Street on three separate occasions, hosted by three different Prime Ministers.

And above all I shall remember feeling proud of being a Welshman who achieved his dream and played rugby for his country. For those who are intent on emphasising the violent aspect of the game and seek something other than the skill and excitement I would simply say, 'Tread softly because you tread on my dreams'.

Appendix

International Appearances and Tries

A. For Wales

Year	Opponents	Venue	Result (Welsh score first)	Tries
1966	Australia	Cardiff	11–14	
1967	England	Cardiff	34–21	2
	France	Paris	14–20	
	Ireland	Cardiff	0–3	
	Scotland	Murrayfield	5–11	
1968	England	Twickenham	11–11	
	Scotland	Cardiff	5–0	
1969	Scotland	Murrayfield	17–3	
	Ireland	Cardiff	24–11	
	France	Paris	8–8	
	New Zealand	Christchurch (1st Test)	0–19	
	New Zealand	Auckland (2nd Test)	12–33	
	Australia	Sydney	19–16	1
1971	England	Cardiff	22–6	2
	France	Paris	9–5	
	Ireland	Cardiff	23–9	2
	Scotland	Murrayfield	19–18	1
1972	England	Twickenham	12–3	
	France	Cardiff	20–6	1

153

Gerald Davies

Year	Opponents	Venue	Result (Welsh score first)	Tries
	Scotland	Cardiff	35–12	1
	New Zealand	Cardiff	16–19	
1973	England	Cardiff	25–9	1
	Scotland	Murrayfield	9–10	
	Ireland	Cardiff	16–12	
	France	Paris	3–12	
	Australia	Cardiff	24–0	1
1974	Scotland	Cardiff	6–0	
	France	Cardiff	16–16	
	England	Twickenham	12–16	
1975	France	Paris	25–10	1
	England	Cardiff	20–4	1
	Scotland	Murrayfield	10–13	
	Ireland	Cardiff	32–4	1
1976	England	Twickenham	21–9	
	Scotland	Cardiff	28–6	
	Ireland	Dublin	34–9	2
	France	Cardiff	19–13	
1977	Ireland	Cardiff	25–9	1
	France	Paris	9–16	
	England	Cardiff	14–9	
	Scotland	Murrayfield	18–9	
1978	England	Twickenham	9–6	
	Scotland	Cardiff	22–14	
	Ireland	Dublin	20–16	
	Australia	Brisbane (1st Test)	8–18	1
	Australia	Sydney (2nd Test)	17–19	1

B. For the British Lions

Year	Opponent	Venue	Result (Lions' score first)	Tries
1968	South Africa	Cape Town (3rd Test)	6–11	
1971	New Zealand	Dunedin (1st Test)	9–3	
	New Zealand	Christchurch (2nd Test)	12–22	2
	New Zealand	Wellington (3rd Test)	13–3	1
	New Zealand	Auckland (4th Test)	14–14	

C. Summary

For Wales: 46 Internationals, of which Wales won 29, lost 14 and drew 3 (points for 758, points against 507). 20 tries, 8 of them before the value of a try was raised to four points in the 1971–72 season (72 points in all).

For the British Lions: 5 Internationals of which the Lions won 2, lost 2 and drew 1 (points for 54, points against 53). 3 tries, all of them before 1971–72 (9 points).

Index